For Caroline and Alexis

Special thanks to

Our parents
Alexis and Mary FitzGerald
for their great encouragement and enthusiasm

Jack Hutchinson
for his support and patience

Alice Brennan
for her long hours and dedication to this book.

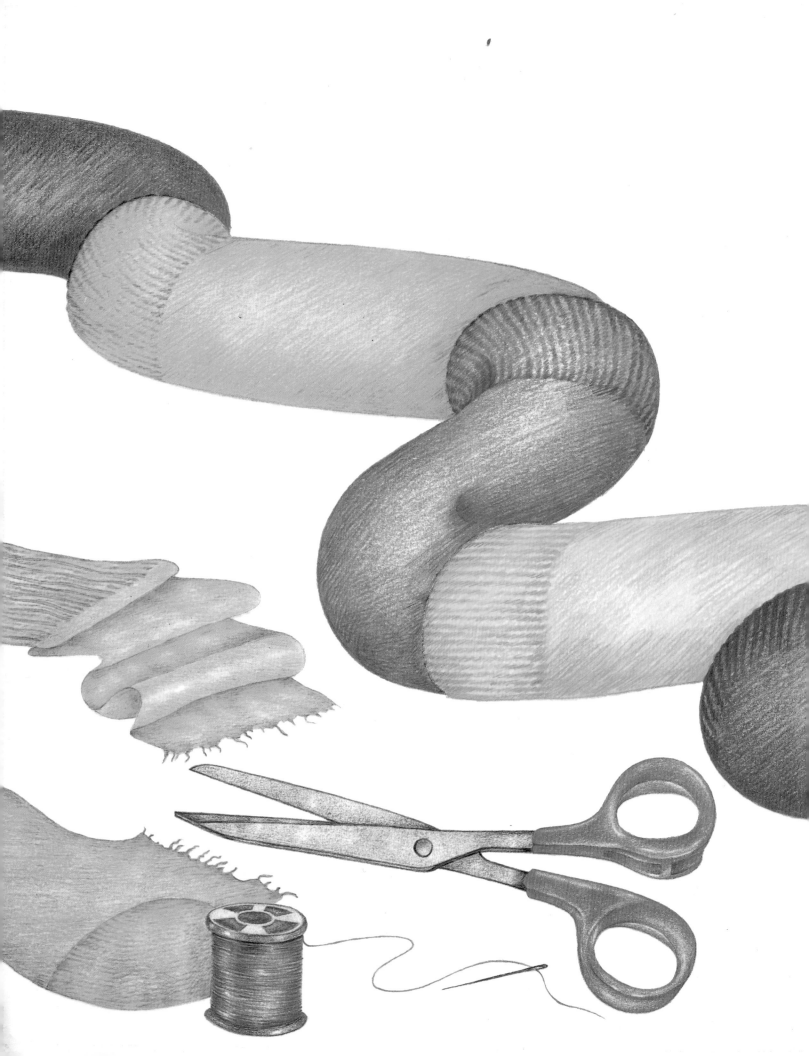

MAKE FOR FUN

MARY FITZGERALD

Illustrated by Jacinta FitzGerald

First published in the UK 1992
by BOXTREE LIMITED, 36 Tavistock Street,
London WC2E 7PB

10 9 8 7 6 5 4 3 2 1

1–85283–669–5

Typeset by Cambrian Typesetters, Frimley
Printed and bound in Great Britain
by Cambus Litho Ltd., East Kilbride, Scotland.

A catalogue record for this book is available
from the British Library

CONTENTS

7 Introduction

9 Clown

11 Helter Skelter

13 Wax Candles

15 Decorated Trainers & Wellies

17 Hobbyhorse

19 Football Game

21 Gift Wrapping

23 Pop-up Cards

25 Fishing Game

27 Doll's Bed & Dressing Table

29 Stained Glass Window

31 Tie & Dye T-shirts

33 Stilts & Telephones

35 Flags & Badges

37 Papier Mâché Fruit & Vegetables

39 Devil's Outfit

41 "Daisy the Cow"

43 Sock Snake

45 Swedish Christmas Decorations

47 Matchbox Dolls

49 Homemade Ice-cream

51 Marzipan Fruits

53 Turtle Cakes

55 Castle Cake

57 Horseboxes

59 Armour

61 Fridge Magnets

63 Shop

64 Helpful Suggestions

INTRODUCTION

Hi!

How would you like a game of football, a spin down a helter skelter or a ride on a hobby horse – or better still, a dish of homemade ice-cream followed by homemade sweets and turtle cakes! You can have these and much more by simply following the easy step by step instructions inside my *Make For Fun* book. In no time at all, you will be able to make these plus your own tie and dye T-shirts, unusual candles, brightly coloured clown and fridge magnets, to name but a few.

Most of the materials you will need can be found in your own kitchen. Felt, brightly coloured paper, glue and some other unusual materials are available in most good craft shops. There are lots of simple suggestions to help you at the back of the book. Try and read these before you start.

So, go on, make the castle cake and crown yourself its King or Queen, dazzle your friends with jazzy trainers and wellies, walk tall with a new pair of stilts or just make pop-up cards to surprise and cheer up your family. It's easy because anything is possible when you make for fun!

YOU WILL NEED

FELT IN DIFFERENT COLOURS

CORN FLAKES

POLYSTYRENE BALL

EGG CUP

10p PIECE

THIN ELASTIC/ HAT ELASTIC

MARKER

CARD OR EMPTY CEREAL BOX

NEEDLE & THREAD

OLD WHITE TIGHTS

COTTON WOOL

SCISSORS

RIBBON

CUP & SAUCER

WOOL

CLOWN

HOW TO MAKE

1 SAUCER · CUP · EGG CUP

On a sheet of card or cereal box use a marker to draw around a saucer to make a big circle. Draw around a cup to make a medium sized circle. Do the same with the 10p piece and an egg cup. Cut out the 4 different sized card circles.

2 Place the big card circle on a piece of felt. Draw around it and cut the felt circle out. Do the same on the other pieces of different coloured felt.

Altogether, cut out 12 big circles of felt for the body. Do the same with the medium sized circle until you have cut out 64 felt circles (14 for each arm and 18 for each leg).

Cut out 4 small felt circles, 2 for the arms and 2 for the feet. Cut out a very small circle for the hat bobble.

3 Sew a running stitch along the edge of each circle.

When complete, pull the thread and the circle should come together. Sew in the centre. Do the same with all the other circles.

4 To make the head, cover the polystyrene ball with a piece of white tights. Sew the tights at the top and bottom of the ball. Cut about 20 strips of wool, 5–6 cm long for hair, and stick around three quarters of the head.

For eyes, cut 4 strips of black felt and stick 2 together to form a cross. Cut a circle of felt for a nose and a small strip of felt for a mouth. Stick these onto the head.

For the hands and feet, place a small cotton wool ball in the centre of each circle before you pull the thread.

Then pull the thread to form a ball and sew in the centre as before.

5 To make the hat, use a saucer to draw a circle on card. Cut out half this and cover it with felt.

Fold it around to make a cone shape, and glue at the edges. Make the bobble for the hat the same way as you made the hands and feet. Sew or glue it on top.

To assemble the clown, thread a darning needle with a long double piece of elastic. Knot it at the end, thread it through the head, then thread on the 12 body circles. Separate the elastic into 2 pieces. On each piece thread on each of the 18 leg circles and a foot piece.

6 For the arms, get a separate piece of elastic and thread on 14 circles and a hand. Tie a bow around the clown's neck and stick or sew the hat on his head.

GLUE

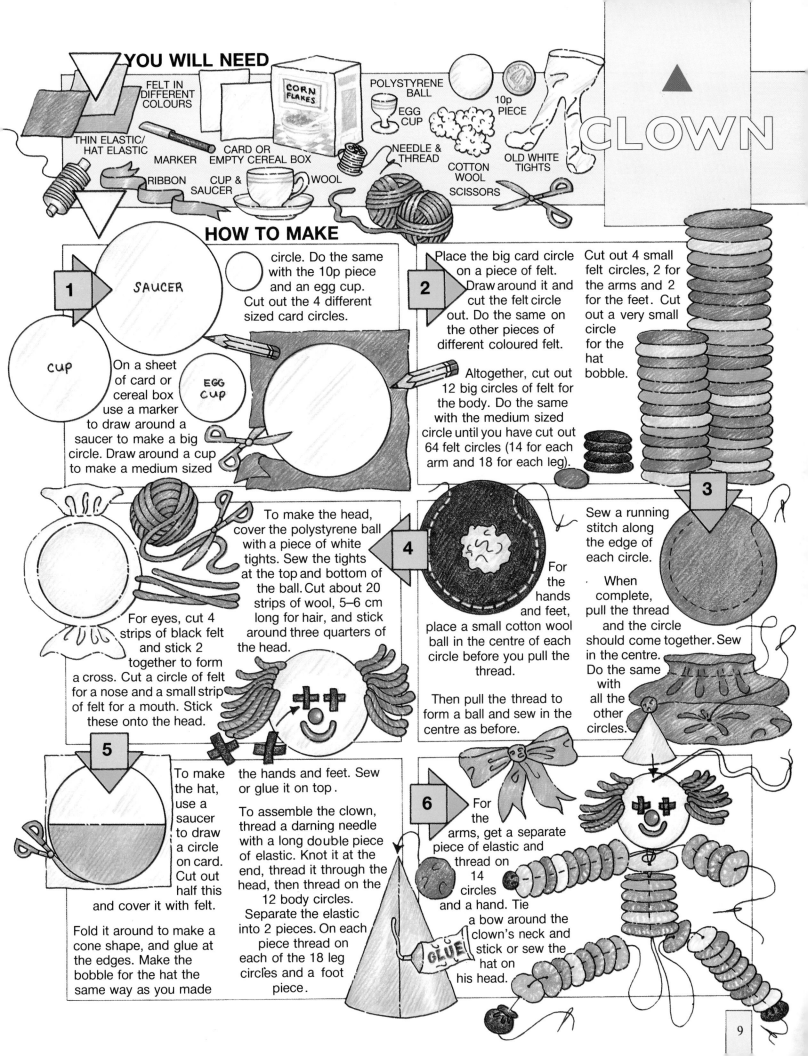

YOU WILL NEED

STRING 38 cm LONG

PENCIL

COTTON REEL

PAINT, MARKERS OR COLOURED PAPER

2–3 SHEETS STRONG CARD

COLOURED STICKY TAPE

GLUE

PLASTICINE

BLUE TACK

VELCRO PADS

SCISSORS

HOW TO MAKE

1

As you move the pencil, the string wraps itself around the reel. The circle gets smaller and smaller, making a spiral.

Tie one end of the string around the cotton reel and the other end around the pencil. Use plasticine to stick the reel in the middle of the sheet of card. Start to draw a circle as though you were using a compass.

2

Fold up the scored edges to make a rim. Make cuts in the rim, as in the diagram, to help it stand up straight.

Cut out the spiral. On the wrong side score a line 1.2 cm from each edge by running the point of your scissors along the card.

3

Cut it out and roll into a cone. Stick the edges together with glue.

To strengthen the rim, stretch strips of coloured sticky tape over the edges. Fold down the tape neatly. On another sheet of card draw a very large quarter-circle.

4

On another sheet of card, draw a quarter-circle that is much smaller than the one you drew in Step 3.

Then draw another quarter-circle that is much smaller than that one. Cut out along the dotted lines.

5

Roll into a cone and stick. Fit upside-down over the pointed cone. Secure with coloured sticky tape or Sellotape. Cut a circle of card a bit bigger than the top of the tower and glue it on.

CUT

6

Cut out windows and a door from coloured paper and stick them onto the tower or draw them on with paint or markers. Stick a velcro pad underneath one end of the spiral and another one on top of the tower. Secure the spiral to the tower with these.

Now see how fast your toy cars can *whizz* down the helter skelter.

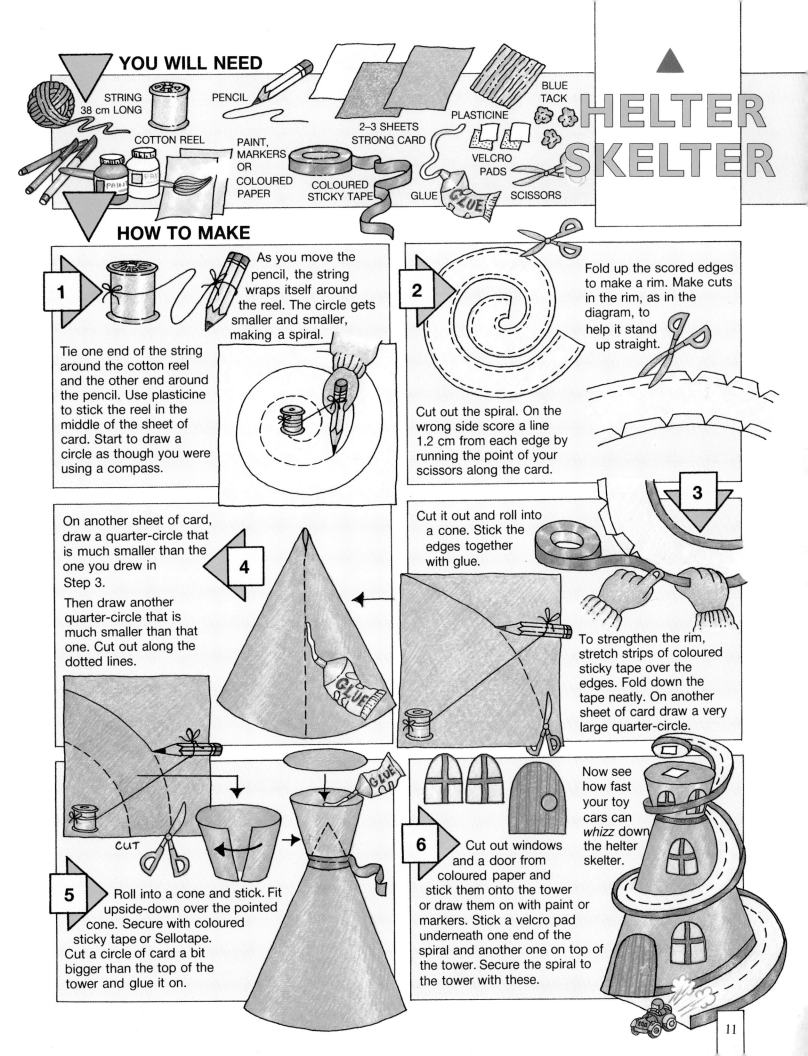

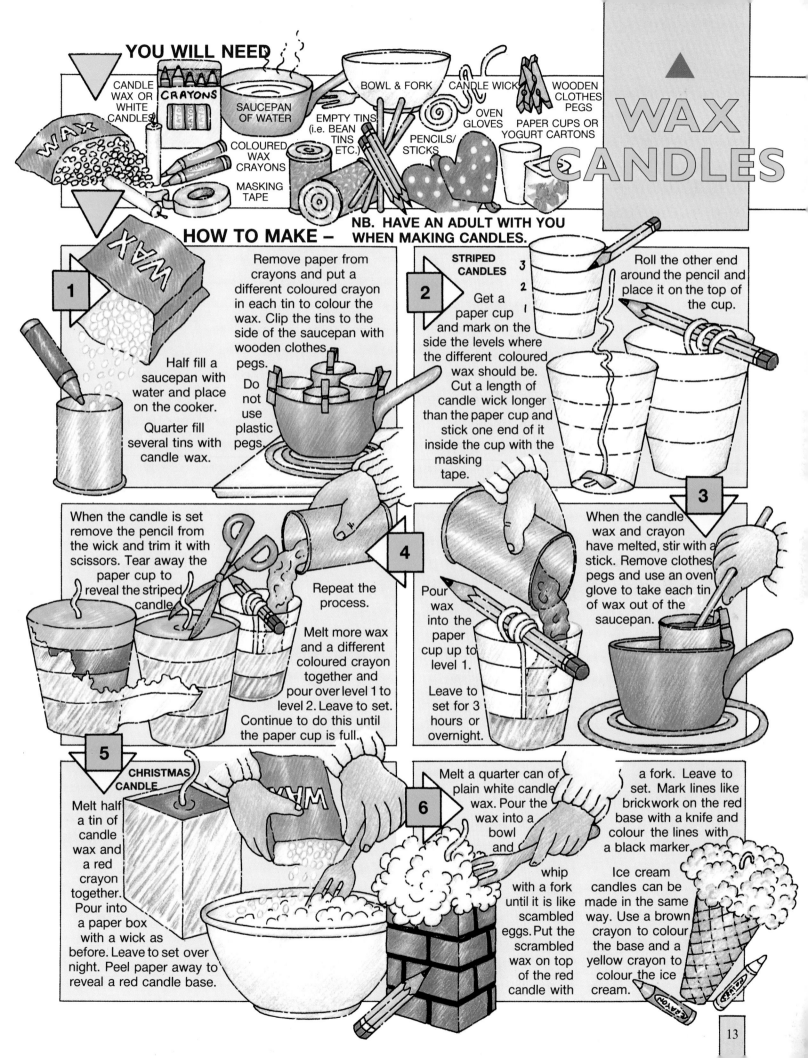

YOU WILL NEED

CANDLE WAX OR WHITE CANDLES

CRAYONS

SAUCEPAN OF WATER

COLOURED WAX CRAYONS

MASKING TAPE

EMPTY TINS (i.e. BEAN TINS ETC.)

BOWL & FORK

CANDLE WICK

PENCILS/STICKS

OVEN GLOVES

WOODEN CLOTHES PEGS

PAPER CUPS OR YOGURT CARTONS

WAX CANDLES

HOW TO MAKE –

NB. HAVE AN ADULT WITH YOU WHEN MAKING CANDLES.

1 Remove paper from crayons and put a different coloured crayon in each tin to colour the wax. Clip the tins to the side of the saucepan with wooden clothes pegs. Do not use plastic pegs.

Half fill a saucepan with water and place on the cooker.

Quarter fill several tins with candle wax.

2 STRIPED CANDLES

Get a paper cup and mark on the side the levels where the different coloured wax should be. Cut a length of candle wick longer than the paper cup and stick one end of it inside the cup with the masking tape.

Roll the other end around the pencil and place it on the top of the cup.

3 When the candle wax and crayon have melted, stir with a stick. Remove clothes pegs and use an oven glove to take each tin of wax out of the saucepan.

4 Repeat the process.

Melt more wax and a different coloured crayon together and pour over level 1 to level 2. Leave to set. Continue to do this until the paper cup is full.

Pour wax into the paper cup up to level 1.

Leave to set for 3 hours or overnight.

When the candle is set remove the pencil from the wick and trim it with scissors. Tear away the paper cup to reveal the striped candle.

5 CHRISTMAS CANDLE

Melt half a tin of candle wax and a red crayon together. Pour into a paper box with a wick as before. Leave to set over night. Peel paper away to reveal a red candle base.

6 Melt a quarter can of plain white candle wax. Pour the wax into a bowl and whip with a fork until it is like scambled eggs. Put the scrambled wax on top of the red candle with a fork. Leave to set. Mark lines like brickwork on the red base with a knife and colour the lines with a black marker.

Ice cream candles can be made in the same way. Use a brown crayon to colour the base and a yellow crayon to colour the ice cream.

13

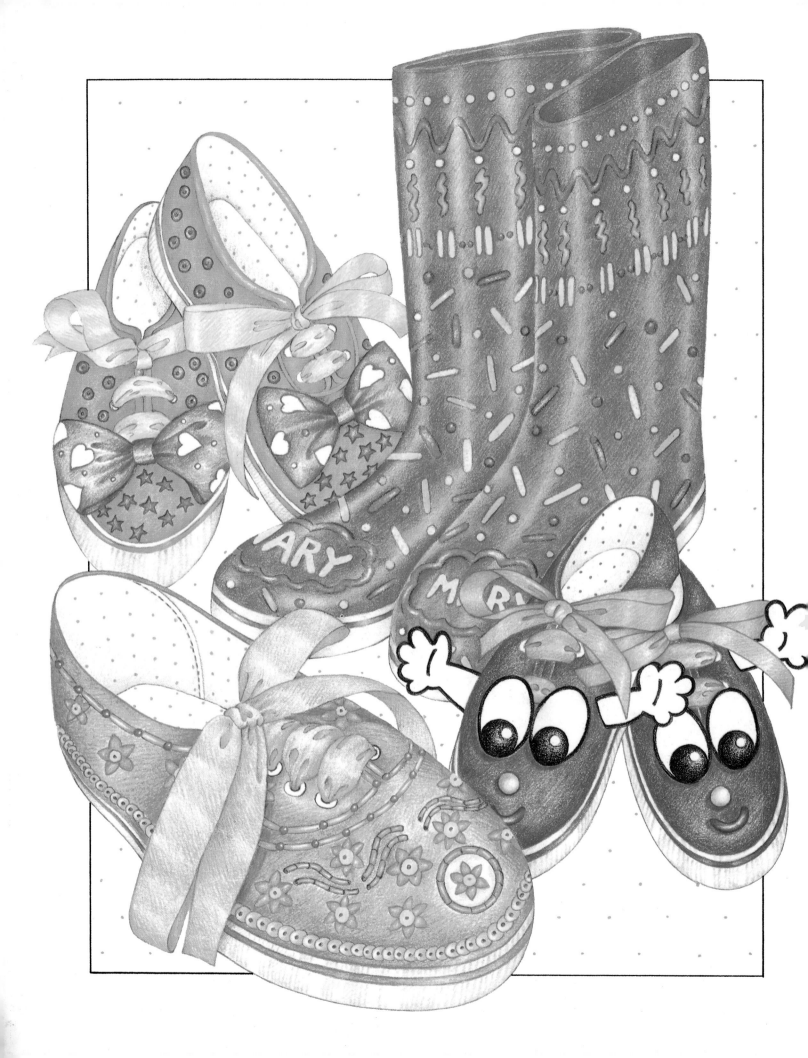

YOU WILL NEED

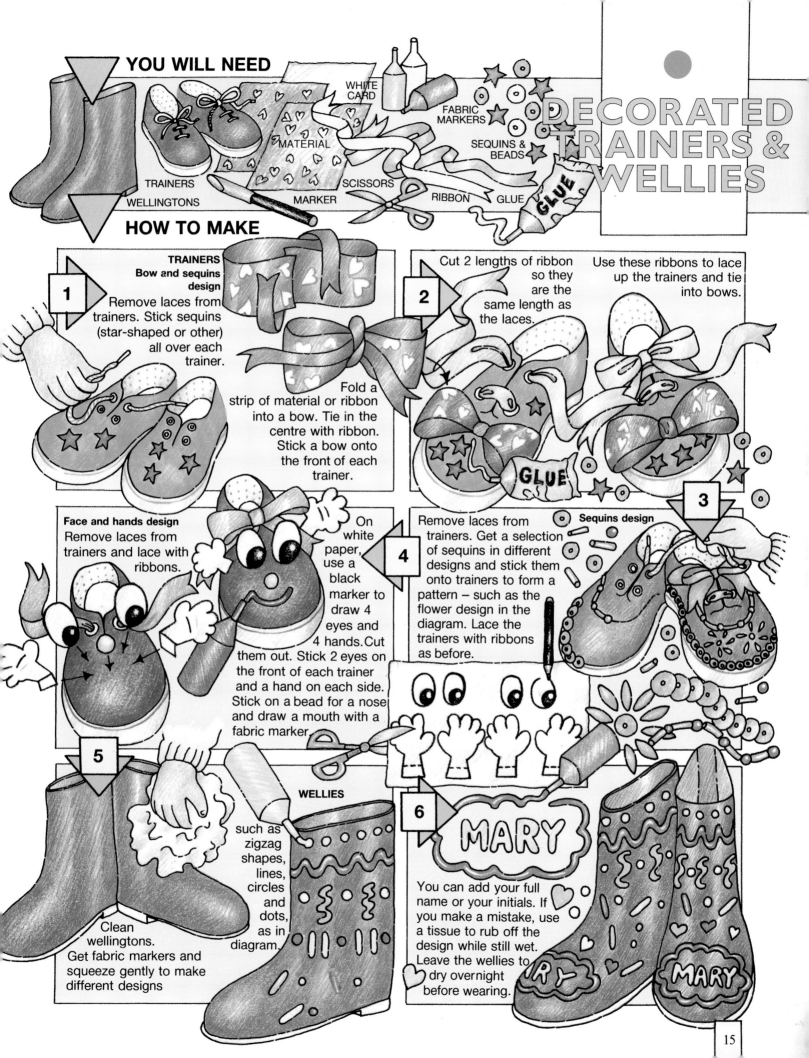

TRAINERS
WELLINGTONS
MARKER
MATERIAL
WHITE CARD
SCISSORS
FABRIC MARKERS
SEQUINS & BEADS
RIBBON
GLUE

HOW TO MAKE

1 TRAINERS
Bow and sequins design
Remove laces from trainers. Stick sequins (star-shaped or other) all over each trainer.

Fold a strip of material or ribbon into a bow. Tie in the centre with ribbon. Stick a bow onto the front of each trainer.

2 Cut 2 lengths of ribbon so they are the same length as the laces. Use these ribbons to lace up the trainers and tie into bows.

Face and hands design
Remove laces from trainers and lace with ribbons.

4 On white paper, use a black marker to draw 4 eyes and 4 hands. Cut them out. Stick 2 eyes on the front of each trainer and a hand on each side. Stick on a bead for a nose and draw a mouth with a fabric marker.

Remove laces from trainers. Get a selection of sequins in different designs and stick them onto trainers to form a pattern – such as the flower design in the diagram. Lace the trainers with ribbons as before.

3 Sequins design

5 Clean wellingtons. Get fabric markers and squeeze gently to make different designs such as zigzag shapes, lines, circles and dots, as in diagram.

WELLIES

6 MARY
You can add your full name or your initials. If you make a mistake, use a tissue to rub off the design while still wet. Leave the wellies to dry overnight before wearing.

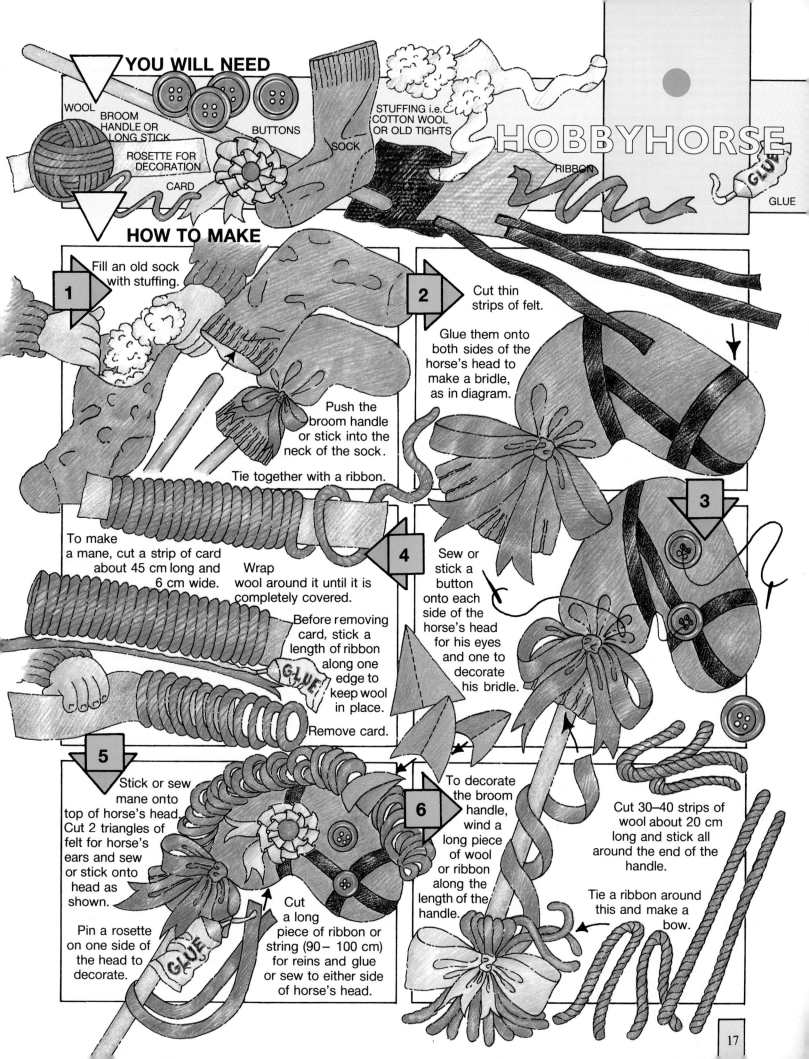

YOU WILL NEED

WOOL

BROOM HANDLE OR LONG STICK

BUTTONS

SOCK

STUFFING i.e. COTTON WOOL OR OLD TIGHTS

RIBBON

GLUE

ROSETTE FOR DECORATION

CARD

HOBBYHORSE

HOW TO MAKE

1 Fill an old sock with stuffing.

Push the broom handle or stick into the neck of the sock.

Tie together with a ribbon.

2 Cut thin strips of felt.

Glue them onto both sides of the horse's head to make a bridle, as in diagram.

3 Sew or stick a button onto each side of the horse's head for his eyes and one to decorate his bridle.

4 To make a mane, cut a strip of card about 45 cm long and 6 cm wide.

Wrap wool around it until it is completely covered.

Before removing card, stick a length of ribbon along one edge to keep wool in place.

GLUE

Remove card.

5 Stick or sew mane onto top of horse's head. Cut 2 triangles of felt for horse's ears and sew or stick onto head as shown.

Pin a rosette on one side of the head to decorate.

GLUE

Cut a long piece of ribbon or string (90 – 100 cm) for reins and glue or sew to either side of horse's head.

6 To decorate the broom handle, wind a long piece of wool or ribbon along the length of the handle.

Cut 30–40 strips of wool about 20 cm long and stick all around the end of the handle.

Tie a ribbon around this and make a bow.

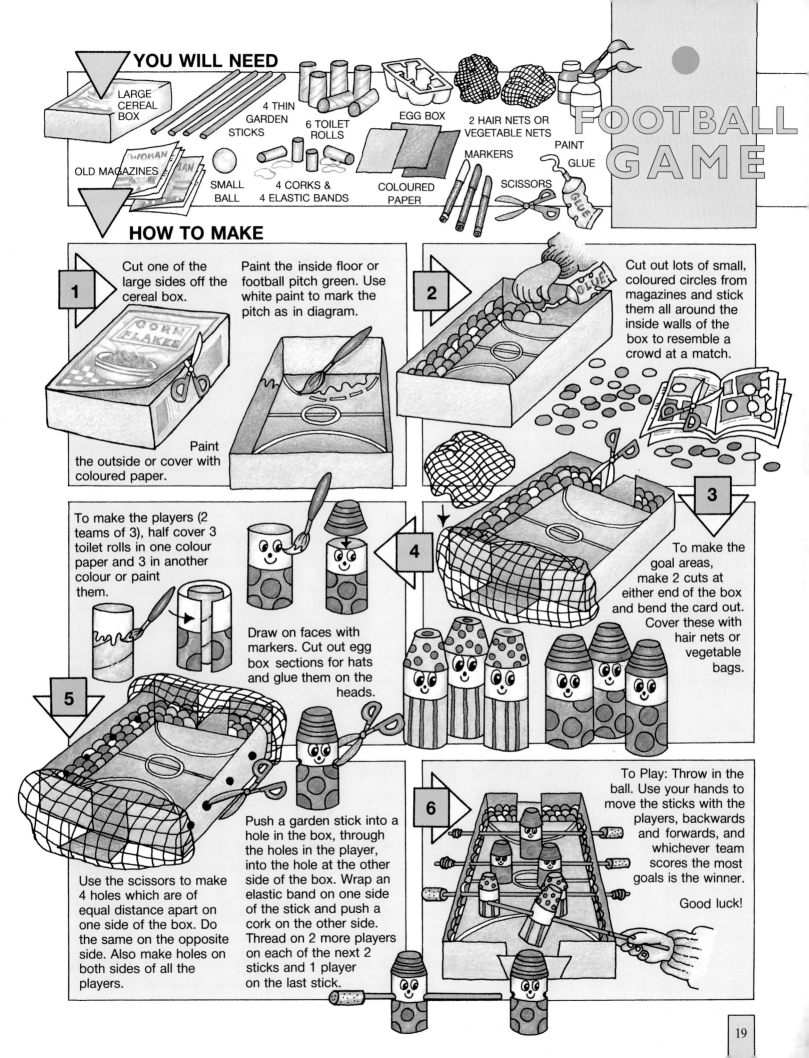

YOU WILL NEED

LARGE CEREAL BOX

4 THIN GARDEN STICKS

6 TOILET ROLLS

EGG BOX

2 HAIR NETS OR VEGETABLE NETS

OLD MAGAZINES

SMALL BALL

4 CORKS & 4 ELASTIC BANDS

COLOURED PAPER

MARKERS

SCISSORS

PAINT

GLUE

HOW TO MAKE

1 Cut one of the large sides off the cereal box.

Paint the inside floor or football pitch green. Use white paint to mark the pitch as in diagram.

Paint the outside or cover with coloured paper.

2 Cut out lots of small, coloured circles from magazines and stick them all around the inside walls of the box to resemble a crowd at a match.

3 To make the goal areas, make 2 cuts at either end of the box and bend the card out. Cover these with hair nets or vegetable bags.

To make the players (2 teams of 3), half cover 3 toilet rolls in one colour paper and 3 in another colour or paint them.

4 Draw on faces with markers. Cut out egg box sections for hats and glue them on the heads.

5 Use the scissors to make 4 holes which are of equal distance apart on one side of the box. Do the same on the opposite side. Also make holes on both sides of all the players.

Push a garden stick into a hole in the box, through the holes in the player, into the hole at the other side of the box. Wrap an elastic band on one side of the stick and push a cork on the other side. Thread on 2 more players on each of the next 2 sticks and 1 player on the last stick.

6 To Play: Throw in the ball. Use your hands to move the sticks with the players, backwards and forwards, and whichever team scores the most goals is the winner.

Good luck!

YOU WILL NEED

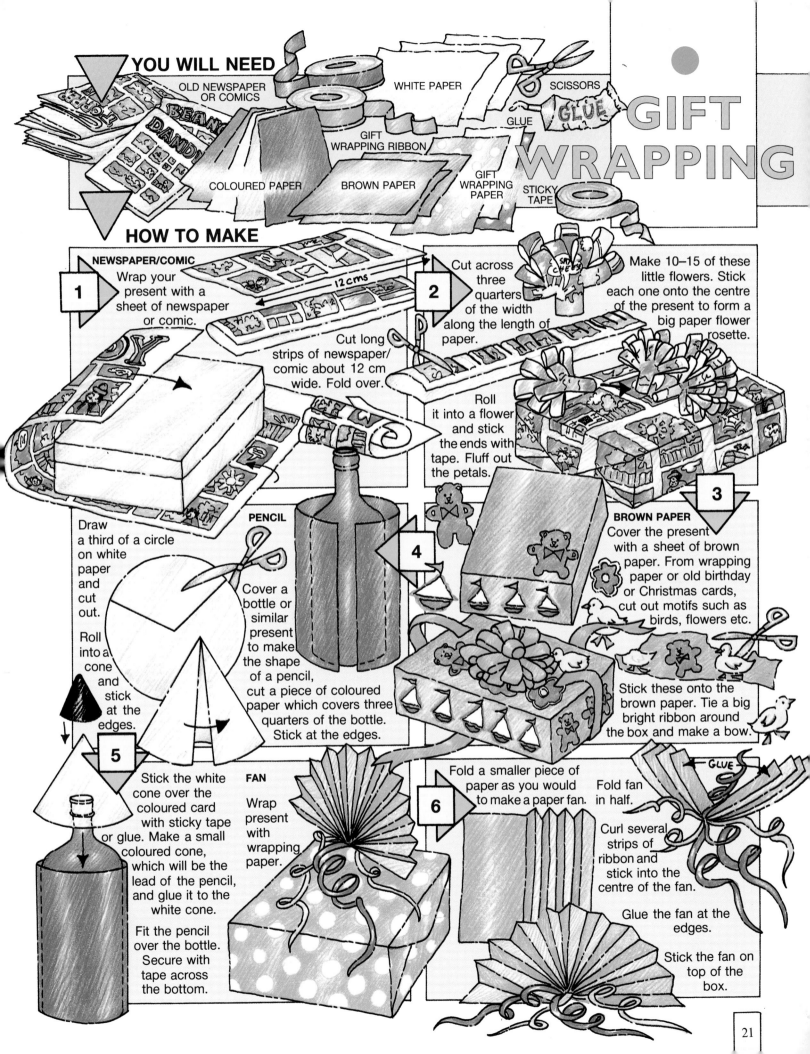

OLD NEWSPAPER OR COMICS

WHITE PAPER

SCISSORS

GLUE

GIFT WRAPPING RIBBON

COLOURED PAPER

BROWN PAPER

GIFT WRAPPING PAPER

STICKY TAPE

GIFT WRAPPING

HOW TO MAKE

NEWSPAPER/COMIC

1 Wrap your present with a sheet of newspaper or comic.

12 cms

Cut long strips of newspaper/comic about 12 cm wide. Fold over.

2 Cut across three quarters of the width along the length of paper.

Roll it into a flower and stick the ends with tape. Fluff out the petals.

Make 10–15 of these little flowers. Stick each one onto the centre of the present to form a big paper flower rosette.

3

BROWN PAPER

Cover the present with a sheet of brown paper. From wrapping paper or old birthday or Christmas cards, cut out motifs such as birds, flowers etc.

Stick these onto the brown paper. Tie a big bright ribbon around the box and make a bow.

Draw a third of a circle on white paper and cut out.

Roll into a cone and stick at the edges.

PENCIL

Cover a bottle or similar present to make the shape of a pencil, cut a piece of coloured paper which covers three quarters of the bottle. Stick at the edges.

4

5 Stick the white cone over the coloured card with sticky tape or glue. Make a small coloured cone, which will be the lead of the pencil, and glue it to the white cone.

Fit the pencil over the bottle. Secure with tape across the bottom.

FAN

Wrap present with wrapping paper.

6 Fold a smaller piece of paper as you would to make a paper fan.

Fold fan in half.

GLUE

Curl several strips of ribbon and stick into the centre of the fan.

Glue the fan at the edges.

Stick the fan on top of the box.

21

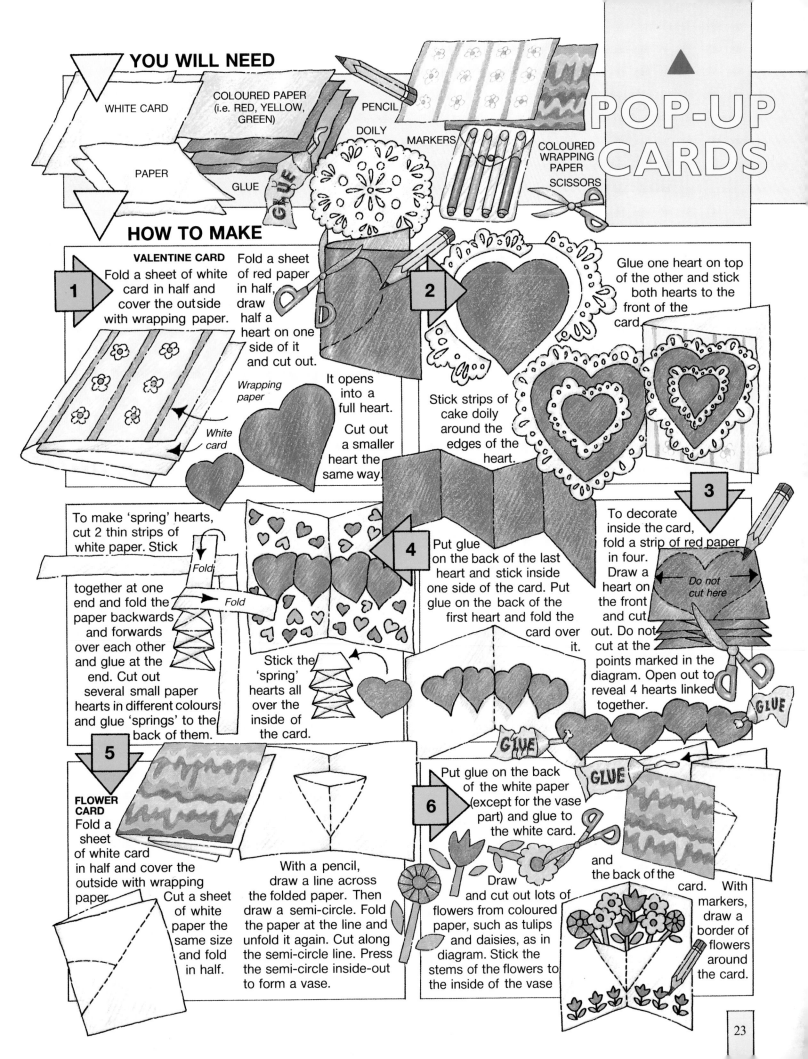

YOU WILL NEED

WHITE CARD

COLOURED PAPER
(i.e. RED, YELLOW, GREEN)

PENCIL

DOILY

MARKERS

COLOURED WRAPPING PAPER

SCISSORS

PAPER

GLUE

HOW TO MAKE

1 VALENTINE CARD
Fold a sheet of white card in half and cover the outside with wrapping paper.

Fold a sheet of red paper in half, draw half a heart on one side of it and cut out.

Wrapping paper

White card

It opens into a full heart.

Cut out a smaller heart the same way.

2 Glue one heart on top of the other and stick both hearts to the front of the card.

Stick strips of cake doily around the edges of the heart.

3 To decorate inside the card, fold a strip of red paper in four. Draw a heart on the front and cut out. Do not cut at the points marked in the diagram. Open out to reveal 4 hearts linked together.

Do not cut here

To make 'spring' hearts, cut 2 thin strips of white paper. Stick together at one end and fold the paper backwards and forwards over each other and glue at the end. Cut out several small paper hearts in different colours and glue 'springs' to the back of them.

Fold

Fold

Stick the 'spring' hearts all over the inside of the card.

4 Put glue on the back of the last heart and stick inside one side of the card. Put glue on the back of the first heart and fold the card over it.

GLUE

GLUE

GLUE

5 FLOWER CARD
Fold a sheet of white card in half and cover the outside with wrapping paper. Cut a sheet of white paper the same size and fold in half.

With a pencil, draw a line across the folded paper. Then draw a semi-circle. Fold the paper at the line and unfold it again. Cut along the semi-circle line. Press the semi-circle inside-out to form a vase.

6 Put glue on the back of the white paper (except for the vase part) and glue to the white card.

Draw and cut out lots of flowers from coloured paper, such as tulips and daisies, as in diagram. Stick the stems of the flowers to the inside of the vase

and the back of the card. With markers, draw a border of flowers around the card.

23

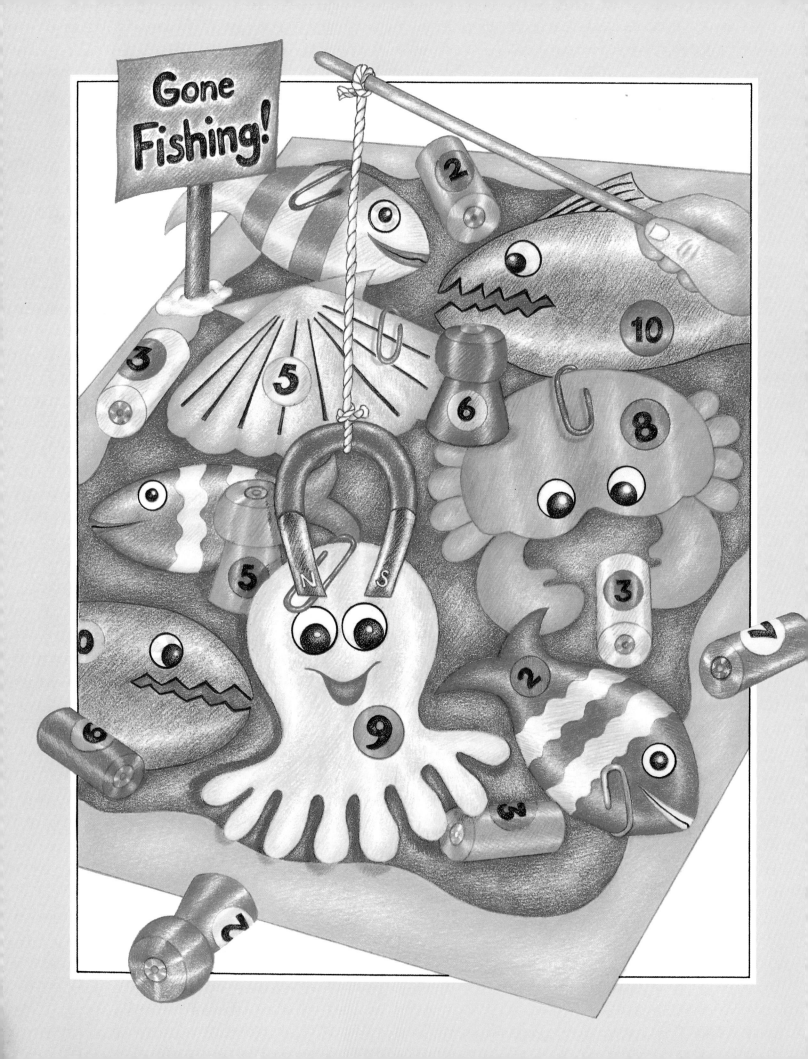

YOU WILL NEED

LARGE SHEET OF CARD

DRAWING PINS

PAPER CLIPS

MAGNET

THIN STICK

PIECE OF FELT

STRING

CORKS

COLOURED PAPER

MARKERS

SCISSORS & GLUE

GLUE

HOW TO MAKE

1 Take a piece of felt which is smaller than the sheet of card and cut into a sea shape.

Stick onto the card.

2 On different pieces of coloured paper, draw and cut out different shaped fish and shells, as in diagram.

Draw eyes and a mouth on both sides of the fish. Make 12–14 fish.

3 Put a paper clip on each fish and write a number on its side.

4 For example, write '10' on the sharks and '2' on the small fish.

Paint the corks different colours and leave to dry. Put a drawing pin in each end of the corks and a number on them too.

5 Make the fishing rod by tying one end of a piece of string to a stick and the other end to a magnet.

6 To Play: Place all the fish and corks in the sea. Each player takes the fishing rod and tries to get a fish or cork out of the sea. If you drop one, pass the rod to the next player.

When all the fish and corks have been removed from the sea, add up your scores.

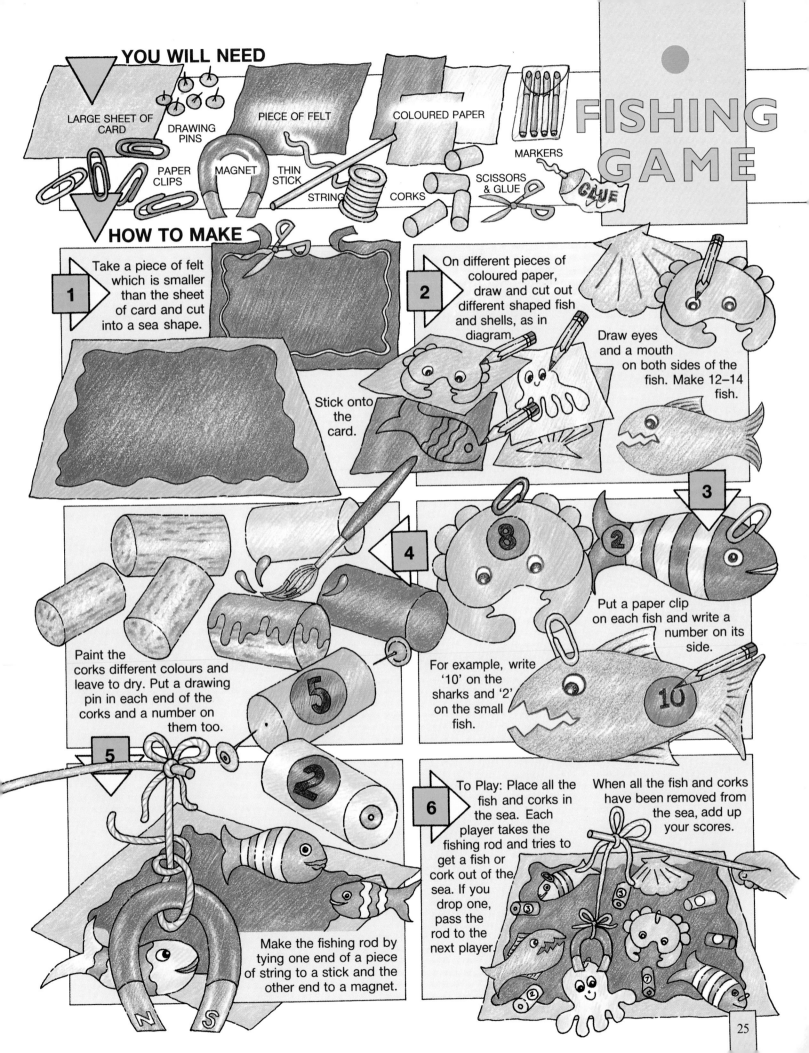

25

YOU WILL NEED

LARGE BOX

6 LARGE MATCHBOXES

TOILET ROLLS

PIECE OF CARD

STICKERS OR MARKERS

4

6 PAPER FASTENERS

COLOURED PAPER

LARGE PIECE OF MATERIAL OR FELT

COTTON WOOL OR OLD TIGHTS

TIN FOIL OR OLD MIRROR

GLUE & SCISSORS

HOW TO MAKE

BED

1 Paint the box or cover with coloured paper.

Make 2 cuts halfway up each of the toilet rolls.

Paint the same colour or cover with the same coloured paper.

CUT   CUT   CUT

2 Cut a piece of card for the back of the bed, as in diagram.

Paint or cover with paper.

Slot each toilet roll into the 4 corners of the box. Glue the card to the back of the box. Decorate the box with stickers or a marker.

3 To make a duvet, cut 2 pieces of material or felt three quarters of the size of the box.

Sew together on the wrong side, making sure to leave a small gap.

4 Do the same for a pillow with 2 smaller pieces of material. Place both on the bed.

Now you have a nice cosy bed for your dolls and teddies.

Turn material to right side, stuff with cotton wool or old tights and sew up the gap.

5 **DRESSING TABLE**

Stick 3 large matchboxes to the other 3 matchboxes.

Push in paper fasteners for handles. Cover with coloured paper.

SAFETY Matches SAFETY

SAFETY Matches SAFETY

6 Cut out a piece of card, as in diagram, for the back of the dressing table. Stick on a square of tin foil or old mirror. Glue to the back of the dressing table.

GLUE

Cut a small piece of material for a mat and place between the bed and dressing table.

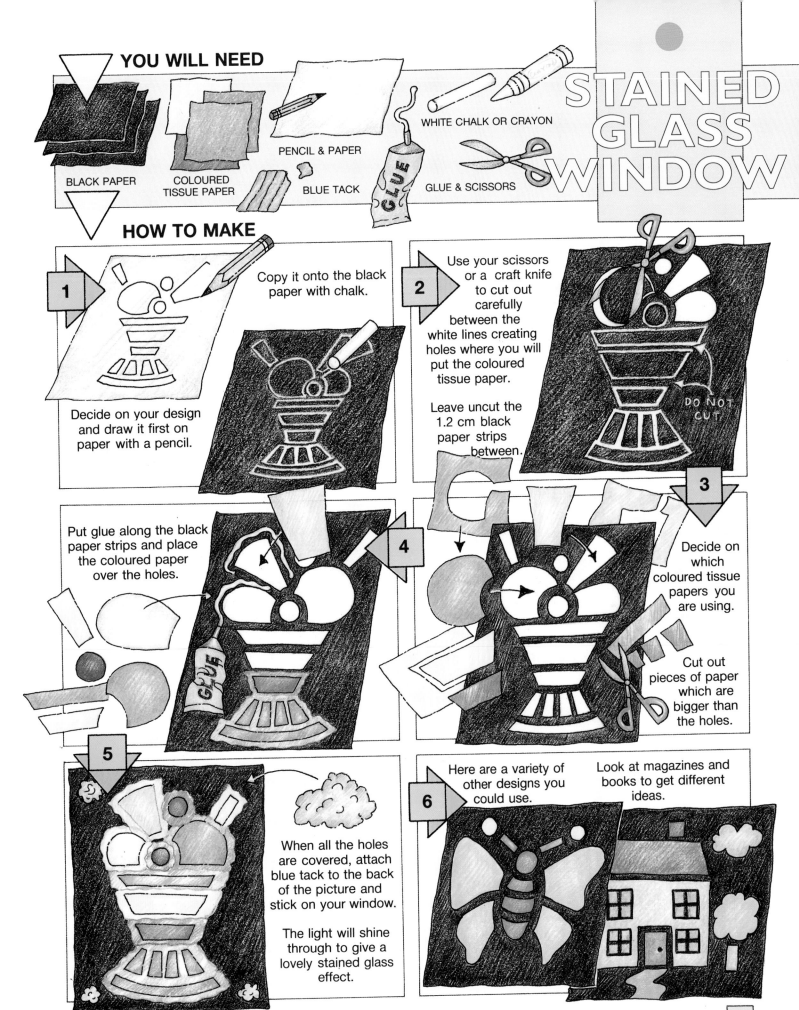

YOU WILL NEED

BLACK PAPER

COLOURED TISSUE PAPER

PENCIL & PAPER

BLUE TACK

GLUE

WHITE CHALK OR CRAYON

GLUE & SCISSORS

STAINED GLASS WINDOW

HOW TO MAKE

1 Copy it onto the black paper with chalk.

Decide on your design and draw it first on paper with a pencil.

2 Use your scissors or a craft knife to cut out carefully between the white lines creating holes where you will put the coloured tissue paper.

Leave uncut the 1.2 cm black paper strips between.

DO NOT CUT

3 Decide on which coloured tissue papers you are using.

Cut out pieces of paper which are bigger than the holes.

4 Put glue along the black paper strips and place the coloured paper over the holes.

5 When all the holes are covered, attach blue tack to the back of the picture and stick on your window.

The light will shine through to give a lovely stained glass effect.

6 Here are a variety of other designs you could use.

Look at magazines and books to get different ideas.

YOU WILL NEED

WHITE COTTON T-SHIRT

DYLON HOT WATER DYES

LARGE BASIN

STRING

WOODEN SPOON OR STICK

PACKET OF SALT

RUBBER GLOVES

TIE & DYE T-SHIRTS

HOW TO MAKE

1 Wash T-shirt and leave damp.

For one T-shirt, you will need a packet of dye, 7 litres hot tap water and 8 tablespoons of salt.

Put on rubber gloves and make up dye in a basin according to instructions on the packet.

2 Decide on what design you would like to tie into your T-shirt.

Here are some ideas:

MARBLING

Scrunch the T-shirt into a ball and tie with string.

3

STONES AND MARBLES

Tie small stones or marbles into the T-shirt, both front and back.

4

SUNBURST

Gather a small piece of the T-shirt in the centre and tie with string. Leave a gap and tie the T-shirt further down. Do this 2 or 3 more times.

PLEATING

Pleat the T-shirt like a paper fan and tie with string at intervals, as in diagram.

5 Place tied T-shirt in basin of dye and stir for the first 15 minutes.

Leave for another 45 minutes, stirring occasionally.

After an hour, remove T-shirt from basin. Rinse in cold water until water runs clear.

Wash in basin of hot water with detergent and rinse again in cold water.

6 Cut out twine and remove stones or marbles if used. Hang up to dry and iron as normal.

Clothes made of natural fabrics such as cotton, linen or silk can be dyed in the same way.

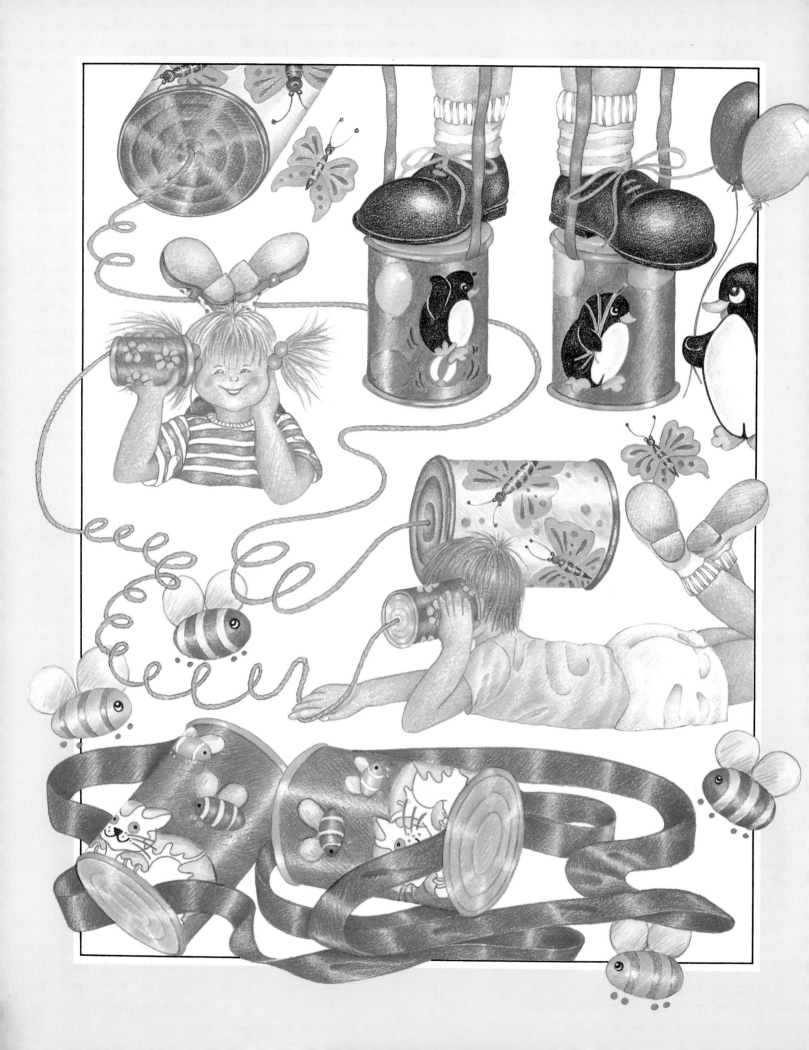

YOU WILL NEED

COLOURED PAPER
(i.e. WRAPPING
PAPER)

WASHING
UP LIQUID

POSTER
PAINT OR
HOUSEHOLD
PAINT &
BRUSHES

GLUE

STRING
OR
RIBBON

SCISSORS

HOW TO MAKE

1 Remove labels from tins.

Wash and dry them.

Paint in primary colours. If using poster or powder paint add a drop of washing up liquid to it so that the paint will stick and not crack on the tin.

2 STILTS

With sharp scissors or a hammer and nail, make a hole at either side of the closed end of the tin.

Cut 2 lengths of string or ribbon 150 cm long.

3 Thread the string through the holes and knot at the ends to secure. To use your stilts, put each foot on a tin and hold the strings with your hands.

Make a hole in the centre of the closed end of each tin.

Thread with string and secure with a knot inside each tin.

TELEPHONES

4 Cut a piece of string 200 cm long.

Now walk and see how tall you are!

5 Give one tin to your friend and hold the other yourself.

Hold taut.

Take it in turns to listen and speak.

Pencils and Paint brushes

6 Tel. Co.

You can decorate your tins by covering them in coloured wrapping paper or draw your own designs, cut out and stick them on the tins.

GLUE

These decorated tins can also be used as pen holders.

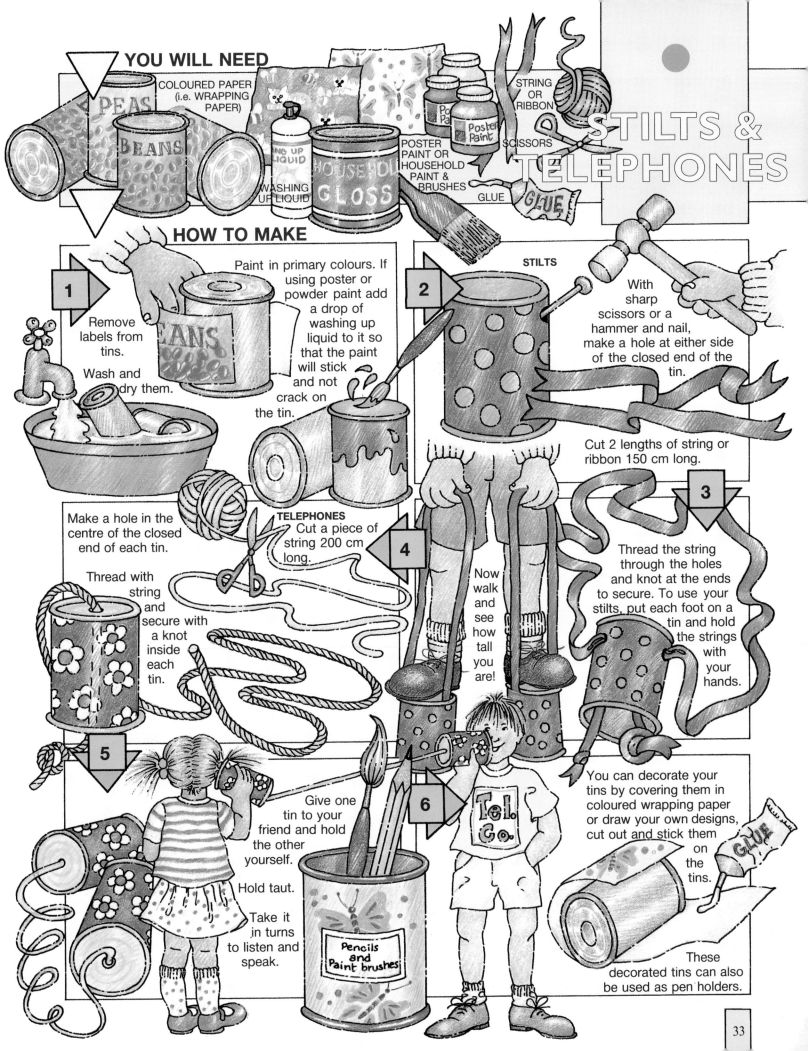

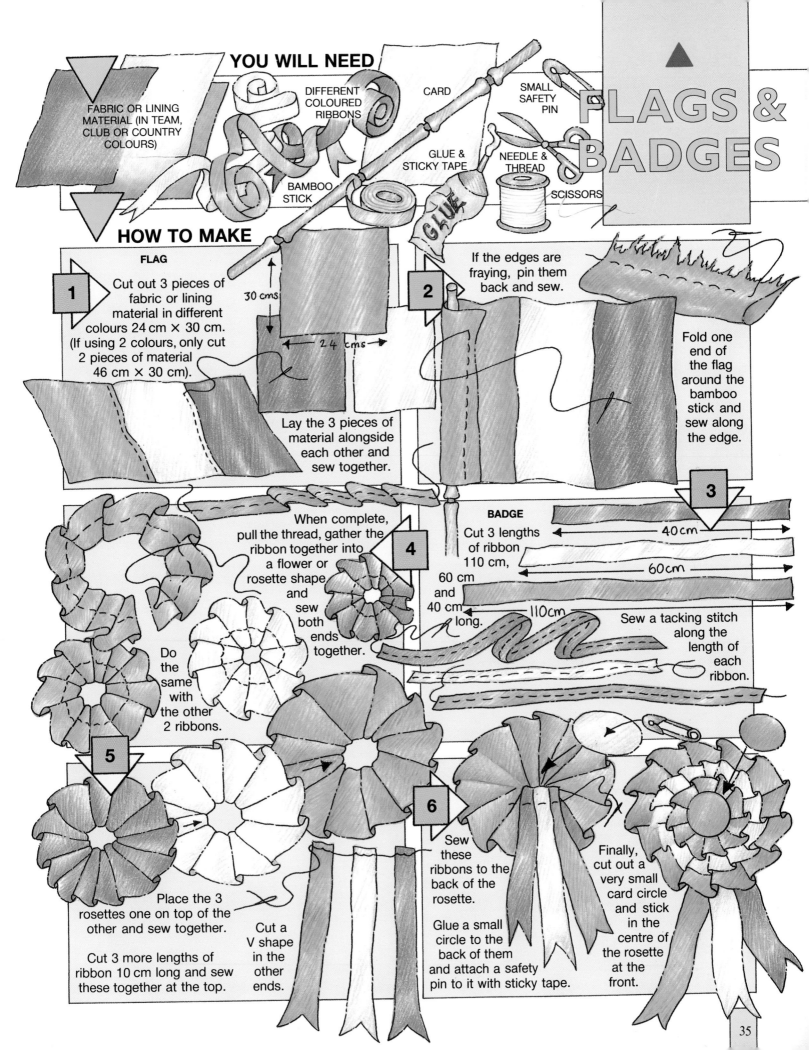

YOU WILL NEED

FABRIC OR LINING MATERIAL (IN TEAM, CLUB OR COUNTRY COLOURS)

DIFFERENT COLOURED RIBBONS

CARD

SMALL SAFETY PIN

BAMBOO STICK

GLUE & STICKY TAPE

NEEDLE & THREAD

SCISSORS

HOW TO MAKE

FLAG

1 Cut out 3 pieces of fabric or lining material in different colours 24 cm × 30 cm. (If using 2 colours, only cut 2 pieces of material 46 cm × 30 cm).

30 cms

24 cms

Lay the 3 pieces of material alongside each other and sew together.

2 If the edges are fraying, pin them back and sew.

Fold one end of the flag around the bamboo stick and sew along the edge.

BADGE

3 Cut 3 lengths of ribbon 110 cm, 60 cm and 40 cm long.

40 cm

60 cm

110 cm

Sew a tacking stitch along the length of each ribbon.

4 When complete, pull the thread, gather the ribbon together into a flower or rosette shape and sew both ends together.

Do the same with the other 2 ribbons.

5 Place the 3 rosettes one on top of the other and sew together.

Cut 3 more lengths of ribbon 10 cm long and sew these together at the top.

Cut a V shape in the other ends.

6 Sew these ribbons to the back of the rosette.

Glue a small circle to the back of them and attach a safety pin to it with sticky tape.

Finally, cut out a very small card circle and stick in the centre of the rosette at the front.

YOU WILL NEED

OLD NEWSPAPERS

BASIN & WATER

POSTER PAINTS & BRUSHES

MARKERS

COLOURED PAPER

BALLOON

Wall paper PASTE

SCISSORS

GLUE

PACKET OF WALLPAPER PASTE

HOW TO MAKE

1 Make a basin of wallpaper paste following instructions on the packet.

Tear newspapers into strips and soak in wallpaper paste to make papier mâché.

To make a banana, squash a sheet of newspaper into a banana shape and cover with a layer of papier mâché.

2 Leave to dry for a day.

Paint yellow and leave to dry again.

Paint on thin brown lines at both ends of the banana. Make 3 or 4 bananas in the same way.

4 For a pineapple, blow up a balloon and cover with several layers of papier mâché. Leave to dry for 2 days.

Leave to dry and decorate the tops with cut out paper leaves and stems.

3 For apples and oranges, squash sheets of newspaper into balls and cover with a layer of papier mâché. Leave to dry overnight.

Paint apples and oranges.

When dry, pierce the pineapple and remove the balloon.

5 Paint the top of the pineapple orange and the bottom yellow. Leave it to dry.

Roll it into a cone and glue at the ends. Cut two V shapes halfway into it and fluff out the leaves. Glue it on top of the pineapple.

6 For pears, squash sheets of newspaper into a pear shape. Cover with a layer of papier mâché and leave to dry. Paint the pears brown. Try making other fruit and vegetables such as tomatoes, strawberries, cucumbers and aubergines.

← 6 cm → 4 cm

For the leaves, cut a strip of green card 6 cm × 4 cm.

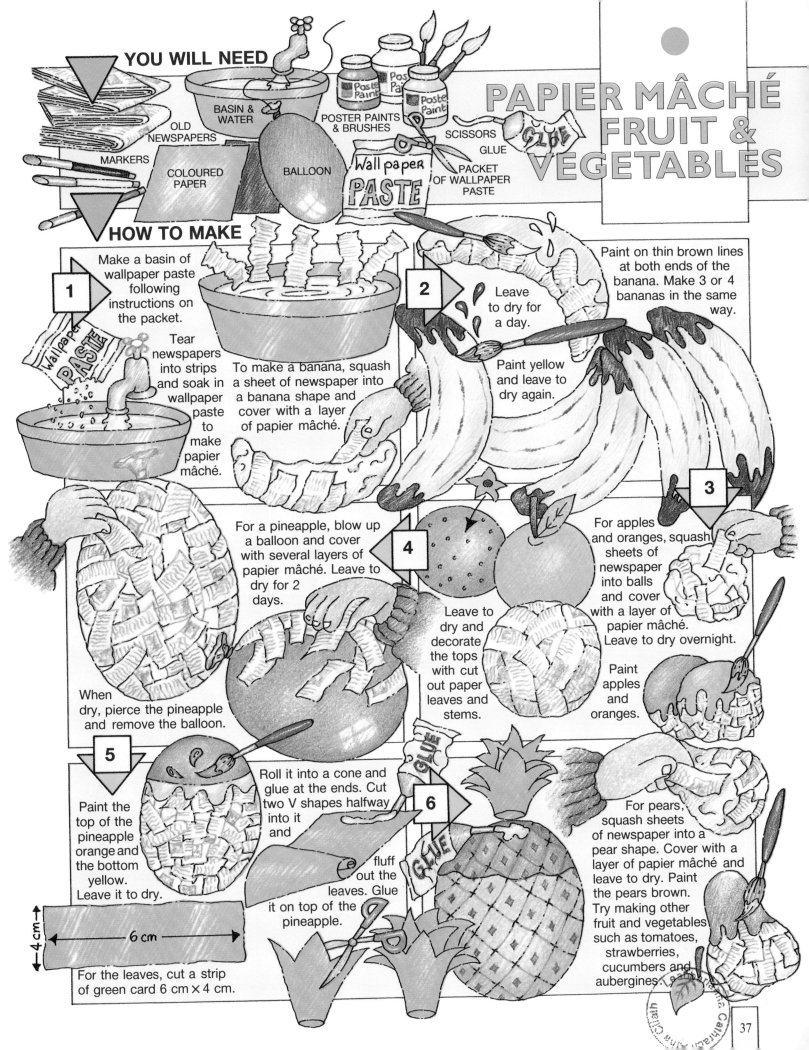

YOU WILL NEED

GLUE
BELT
STAPLER
GARDEN STICK
THIN CARDBOARD
THIN ELASTIC
SCISSORS
STICKY TAPE
TIN FOIL
ROPE OR THICK STRING
RED CARD

DEVIL'S OUTFIT

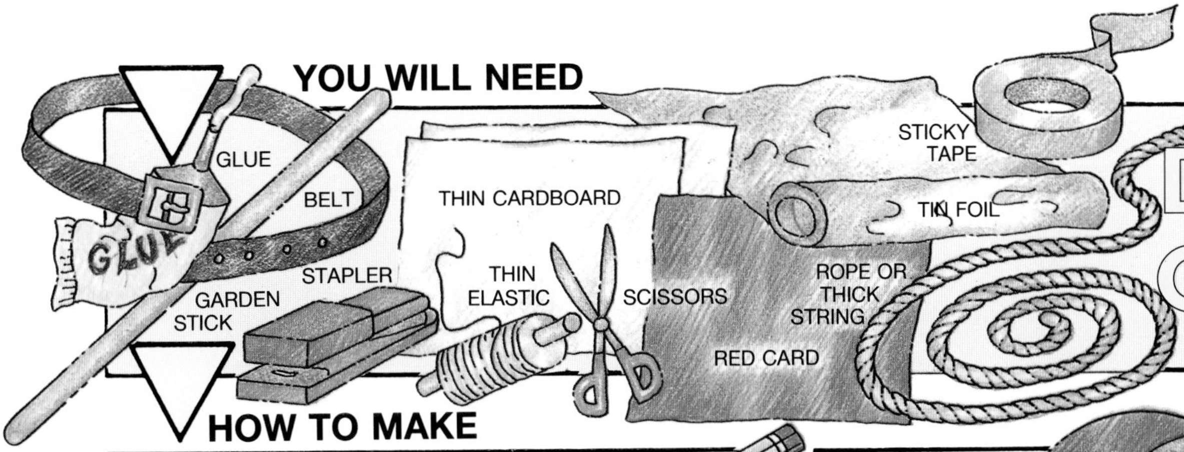

HOW TO MAKE

1 For the devil's ears, place a dinner plate on red card.

Draw around it to make a circle. Cut out.

2 Cut the circle in half.

Make a hole at either side of each cone with scissors.

Thread a piece of elastic, to fit around your head, through these holes and tie.

Fold each half into a cone and fasten with a stapler or sticky tape.

3 For the tail, fold one end of the rope into a small loop and fasten with sticky tape.

4 Draw an arrowhead on red card, cut out and stick to the other end of the rope.

To wear the tail, put a belt through the loop and fasten around your waist.

5 Now draw a three-pronged fork on cardboard and cut it out. Use sticky tape to attach it to the garden stick.

6 Wear red or black clothes when dressing up as a devil!

Tear strips of tin foil and wrap around the stick and fork until they are completely covered.

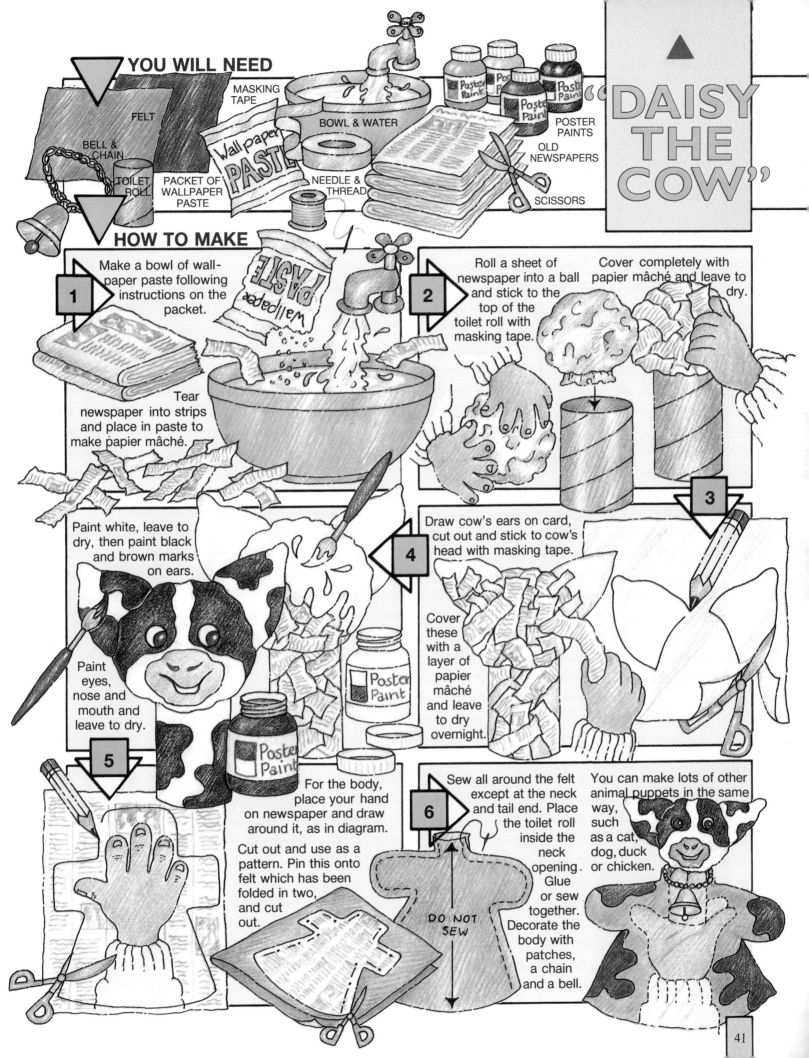

YOU WILL NEED

FELT

MASKING TAPE

BOWL & WATER

POSTER PAINTS

OLD NEWSPAPERS

BELL & CHAIN

TOILET ROLL

PACKET OF WALLPAPER PASTE

Wallpaper PASTE

NEEDLE & THREAD

SCISSORS

HOW TO MAKE

1 Make a bowl of wallpaper paste following instructions on the packet.

Tear newspaper into strips and place in paste to make papier mâché.

2 Roll a sheet of newspaper into a ball and stick to the top of the toilet roll with masking tape. Cover completely with papier mâché and leave to dry.

3 Draw cow's ears on card, cut out and stick to cow's head with masking tape.

Cover these with a layer of papier mâché and leave to dry overnight.

4 Paint white, leave to dry, then paint black and brown marks on ears.

Paint eyes, nose and mouth and leave to dry.

5 For the body, place your hand on newspaper and draw around it, as in diagram.

Cut out and use as a pattern. Pin this onto felt which has been folded in two, and cut out.

6 Sew all around the felt except at the neck and tail end. Place the toilet roll inside the neck opening. Glue or sew together. Decorate the body with patches, a chain and a bell.

DO NOT SEW

You can make lots of other animal puppets in the same way, such as a cat, dog, duck or chicken.

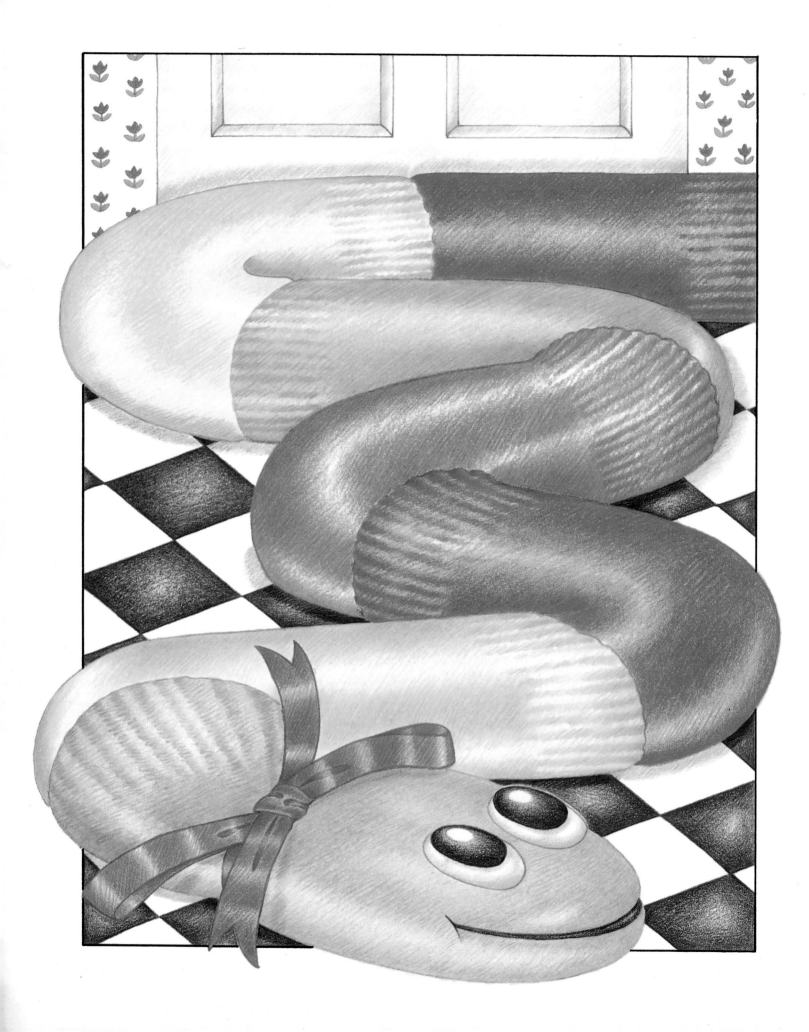

YOU WILL NEED

6–7 ODD SOCKS (COLOURED)

BLACK MARKER OR PAPER

STUFFING (i.e. TOY STUFFING, OLD TIGHTS OR COTTON WOOL)

TABLE TENNIS BALL

SCRAPS OF FELT

SCISSORS

RIBBON

NEEDLE & THREAD

GLUE

SOCK SNAKE

HOW TO MAKE

1 Cut the heel end off 4 or 5 odd socks and keep the leg parts.

With a needle and thread, sew one leg part to the end of a complete sock.

Stuff these two completely with stuffing.

2 Sew another leg part on the end of the last one and stuff again.

Continue to sew on the other 2 or 3 leg parts in the same way making sure to stuff them each time.

3

To make eyes, use a craft knife to cut a table tennis ball in half.

4 Stick a small black circle of paper on each half ball or draw the circles on with a black marker.

Stuff the last complete sock and sew it onto the end of the last sewn-on leg part.

5 Stick the eyes onto the snake's head.

Cut out a thin piece of black felt for a mouth and glue on.

Decorate the snake by tying ribbon at intervals along the length of its body.

Roll up and use as a toy to decorate your bed

6 or place the snake in front of the door to stop draughts.

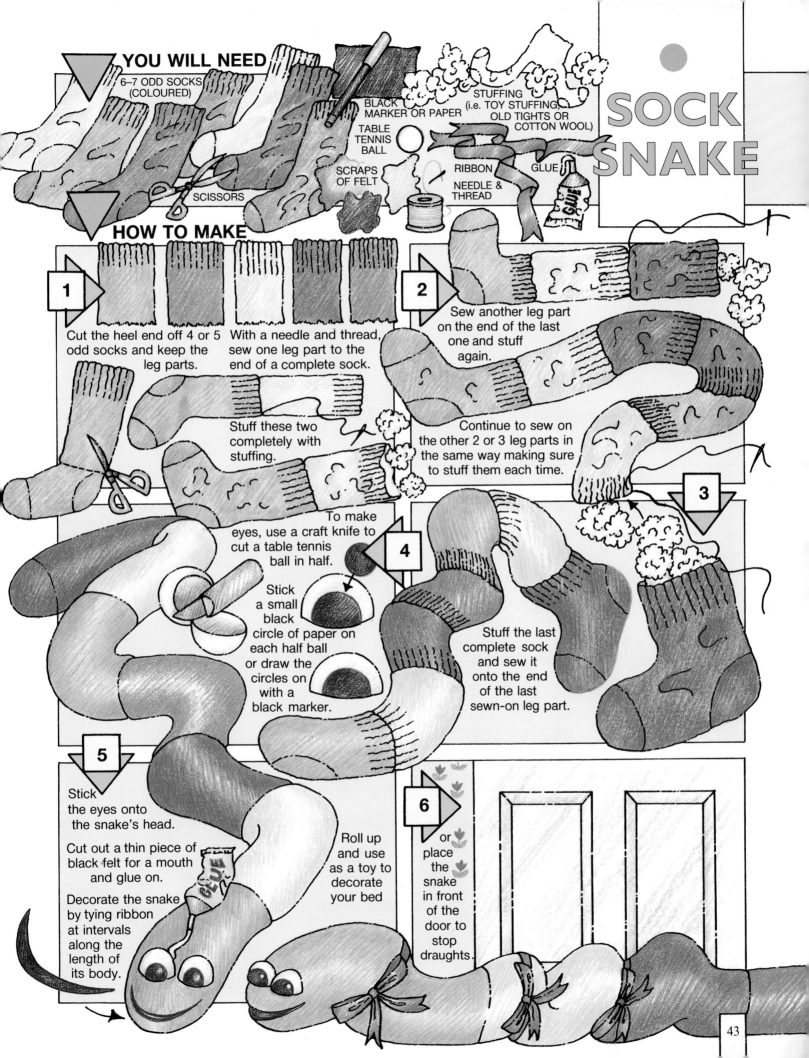

43

YOU WILL NEED

CREPE PAPER OR PLASTIC SHINY PAPER

SEVERAL SHEETS OF COLOURED PAPER (i.e. GREEN, RED, YELLOW AND WHITE)

GLUE

SCISSORS

EMBROIDERY THREAD

CARD

PENCIL & RUBBER

HOW TO MAKE

HEART-SHAPED BASKET

1 On card, draw a curved 'racetrack'. Cut it out and use as a pattern.

Place it on paper, draw around it with a pencil and cut out. Do the same on different coloured paper.

2 Fold each one in half. Make 3 cuts, across three quarters of the width.

Weave the 2 pieces together.

Cut a long strip of paper, 12 cm × 2 cm, for a handle and stick inside either side of the basket.

3

ROUND BASKET

Draw a small circle about the size of a cup on a piece of paper. Draw lots of lines like rays of the sun from it.

4 Cut out and bend up each of these 'rays'.

Cut 5 strips of paper in different colours 12–15 cm × 1.5 cm. Weave 3 of these in and out of the 'rays'.

Glue at the end. Stick the fourth one around the top of the basket and the fifth one, attach as a handle.

SWEDISH HOUSE

On a sheet of paper, draw a house shape, as in diagram. Fold on the dotted lines and glue at the edges.

Cut out windows and a door from coloured paper and stick on either side of the house.

Glue on a handle.

5 Fill the house and baskets with shredded crepe paper or shiny plastic paper.

6

STAR

Cut out 2 triangles in different colours. Put one cut in each triangle and insert one into the other. Glue at the edges.

Make a hole in the top of the star and insert thread.

CHRISTMAS TREE

Fold a long piece of green paper in half. Draw 2 half Christmas trees along the fold. Cut out and open out.

Make a cut half way along the length of each tree, as in diagram. Slot one tree into the other and stick a small star on top. Hang on tree with thread.

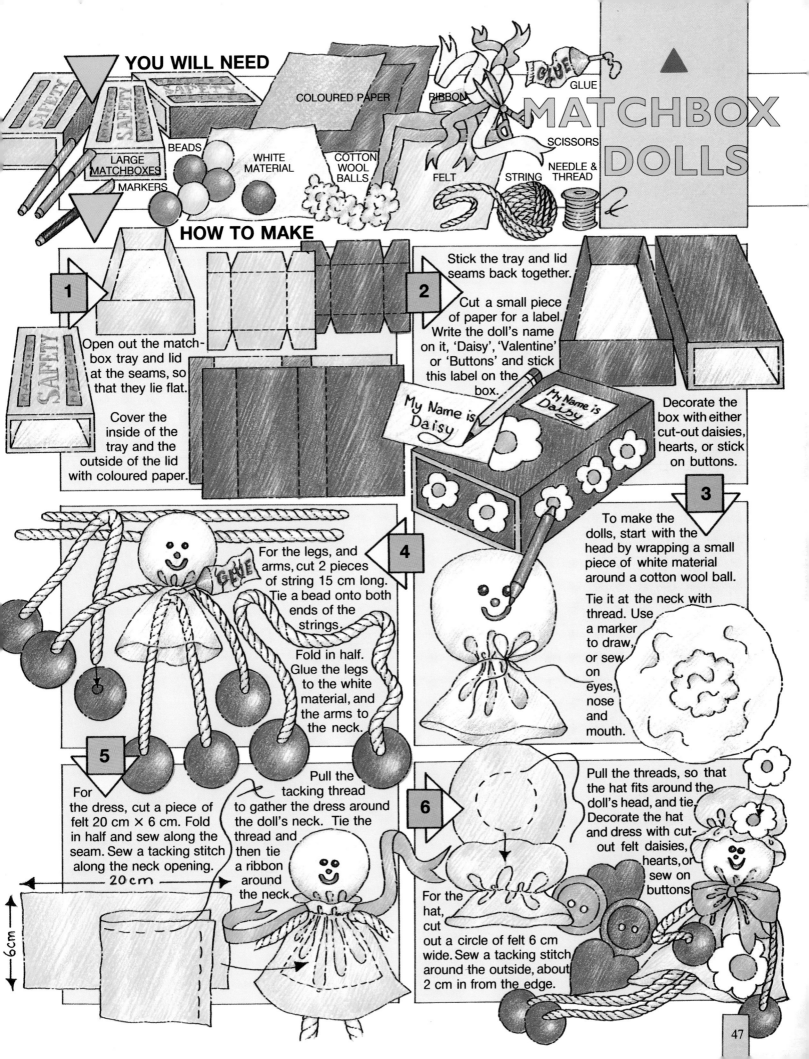

YOU WILL NEED

COLOURED PAPER

RIBBON

GLUE

BEADS

WHITE MATERIAL

COTTON WOOL BALLS

LARGE MATCHBOXES

MARKERS

SCISSORS

FELT

STRING

NEEDLE & THREAD

MATCHBOX DOLLS

HOW TO MAKE

1 Open out the matchbox tray and lid at the seams, so that they lie flat.

Cover the inside of the tray and the outside of the lid with coloured paper.

2 Stick the tray and lid seams back together.

Cut a small piece of paper for a label. Write the doll's name on it, 'Daisy', 'Valentine' or 'Buttons' and stick this label on the box.

My Name is Daisy

My Name is Daisy

Decorate the box with either cut-out daisies, hearts, or stick on buttons.

3 To make the dolls, start with the head by wrapping a small piece of white material around a cotton wool ball.

Tie it at the neck with thread. Use a marker to draw, or sew on eyes, nose and mouth.

4 For the legs, and arms, cut 2 pieces of string 15 cm long. Tie a bead onto both ends of the strings.

Fold in half. Glue the legs to the white material, and the arms to the neck.

GLUE

5 For the dress, cut a piece of felt 20 cm × 6 cm. Fold in half and sew along the seam. Sew a tacking stitch along the neck opening.

20 cm

6 cm

Pull the tacking thread to gather the dress around the doll's neck. Tie the thread and then tie a ribbon around the neck.

6 For the hat, cut out a circle of felt 6 cm wide. Sew a tacking stitch around the outside, about 2 cm in from the edge.

Pull the threads, so that the hat fits around the doll's head, and tie. Decorate the hat and dress with cut-out felt daisies, hearts, or sew on buttons.

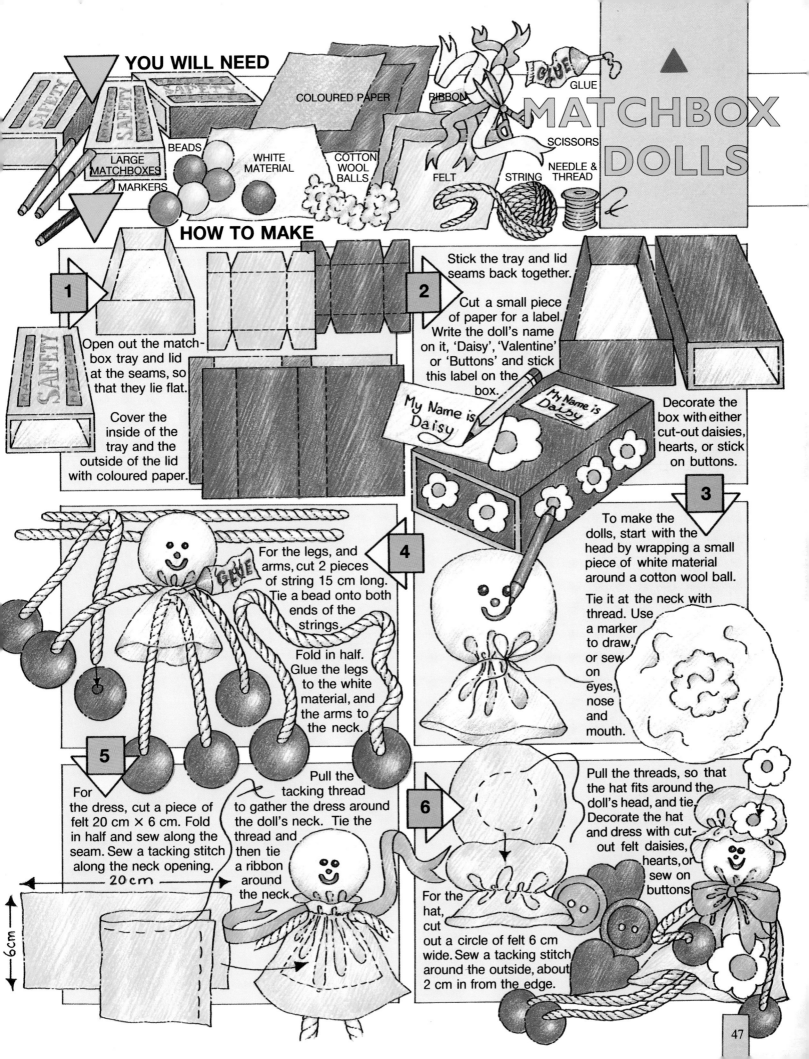

YOU WILL NEED

600 ml (1 PINT) DOUBLE CREAM

175 g (6 oz) CASTER SUGAR

1 TEASPOON VANILLA ESSENCE

HOMEMADE ICE CREAM

HOW TO MAKE

1 Pour the cream into a bowl and whip until thick.

2 Slowly add the caster sugar and mix well.

Add the vanilla essence and mix in.

3

4 Pour the mixture into a small cake tin or ice tray and put in the freezer for an hour. Remove and whisk the mixture again.

Return to the freezer for 3–4 hours until hard.

LEAVE FOR 20 MINUTES

Leave in the lower part of the fridge for about 20 minutes before serving.

FRIDGE

Serve plain with wafers or with chocolate or strawberry sauce.

FREEZER

1 HOUR THEN 3–4 HOURS UNTIL HARD

5 BANANA SPLIT

Cut a banana in half and place in a desert bowl.

Put 2–3 scoops of ice cream on the banana.

Top with chocolate sauce and chopped nuts.

6 KNICKERBOCKER GLORY

Fill a tall glass with layers of ice cream and tinned fruit salad.

Top with strawberry sauce, cream and chocolate flake.

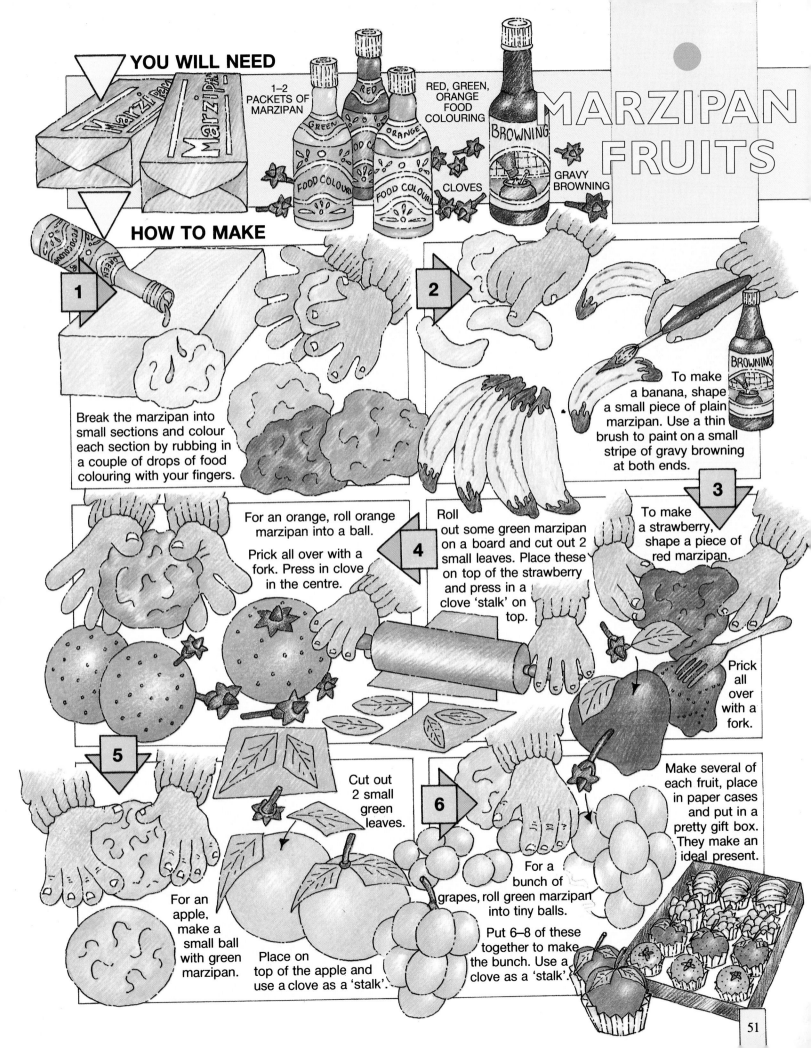

YOU WILL NEED

1–2 PACKETS OF MARZIPAN

RED, GREEN, ORANGE FOOD COLOURING

CLOVES

BROWNING

GRAVY BROWNING

MARZIPAN FRUITS

HOW TO MAKE

1 Break the marzipan into small sections and colour each section by rubbing in a couple of drops of food colouring with your fingers.

2 To make a banana, shape a small piece of plain marzipan. Use a thin brush to paint on a small stripe of gravy browning at both ends.

3 To make a strawberry, shape a piece of red marzipan.

Roll out some green marzipan on a board and cut out 2 small leaves. Place these on top of the strawberry and press in a clove 'stalk' on top.

Prick all over with a fork.

4 For an orange, roll orange marzipan into a ball.

Prick all over with a fork. Press in clove in the centre.

5 For an apple, make a small ball with green marzipan.

Cut out 2 small green leaves.

Place on top of the apple and use a clove as a 'stalk'.

6 For a bunch of grapes, roll green marzipan into tiny balls.

Put 6–8 of these together to make the bunch. Use a clove as a 'stalk'.

Make several of each fruit, place in paper cases and put in a pretty gift box. They make an ideal present.

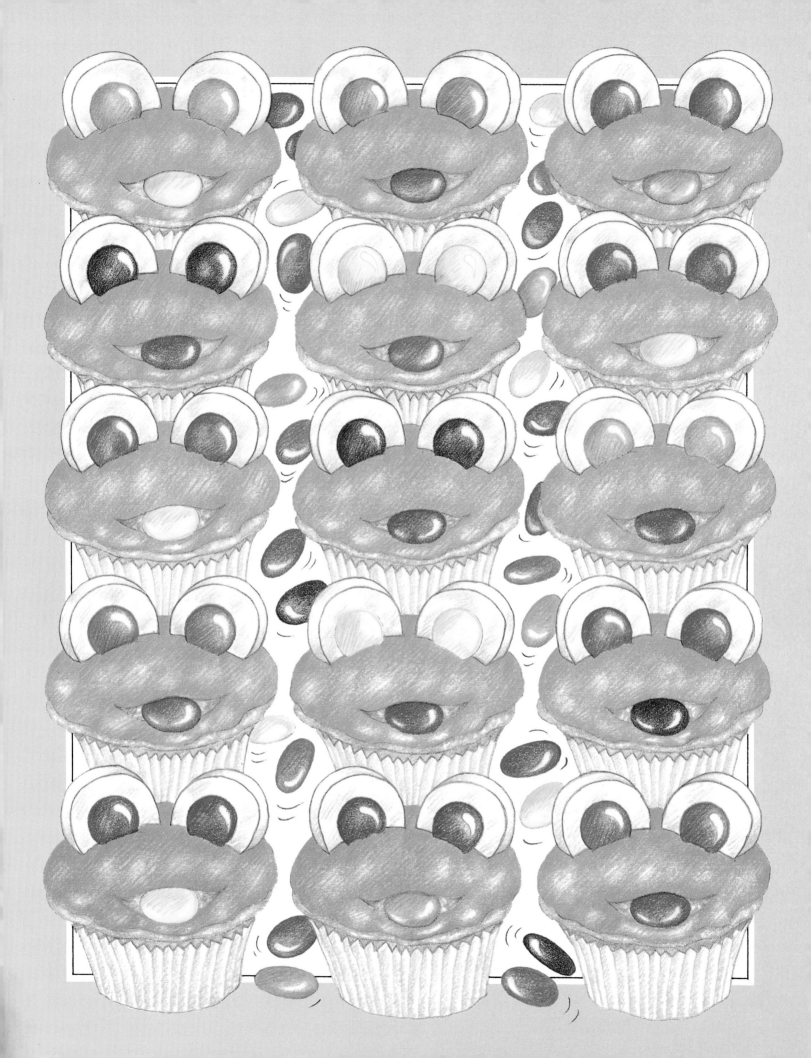

YOU WILL NEED

150 g (6 oz) SELF-RAISING FLOUR

100 g (4 oz) MARGARINE

2 EGGS

100 g (4 oz) CASTER SUGAR

ICING

50 g (2 oz) MARGARINE

GREEN FOOD COLOURING

PAPER CASES

100 g (4 oz) ICING SUGAR

SMARTIES & MARSHMALLOWS TO DECORATE

HOW TO MAKE

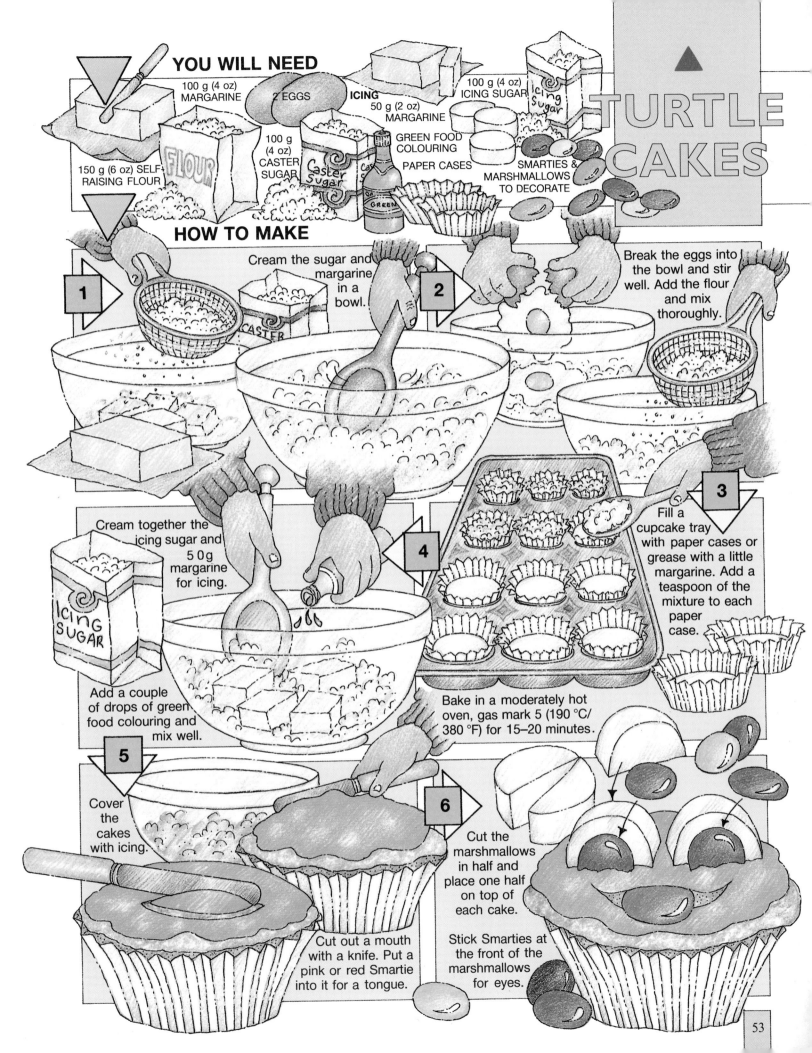

1 Cream the sugar and margarine in a bowl.

2 Break the eggs into the bowl and stir well. Add the flour and mix thoroughly.

3 Fill a cupcake tray with paper cases or grease with a little margarine. Add a teaspoon of the mixture to each paper case.

4 Cream together the icing sugar and 50g margarine for icing.

Add a couple of drops of green food colouring and mix well.

Bake in a moderately hot oven, gas mark 5 (190 °C/380 °F) for 15–20 minutes.

5 Cover the cakes with icing.

Cut out a mouth with a knife. Put a pink or red Smartie into it for a tongue.

6 Cut the marshmallows in half and place one half on top of each cake.

Stick Smarties at the front of the marshmallows for eyes.

53

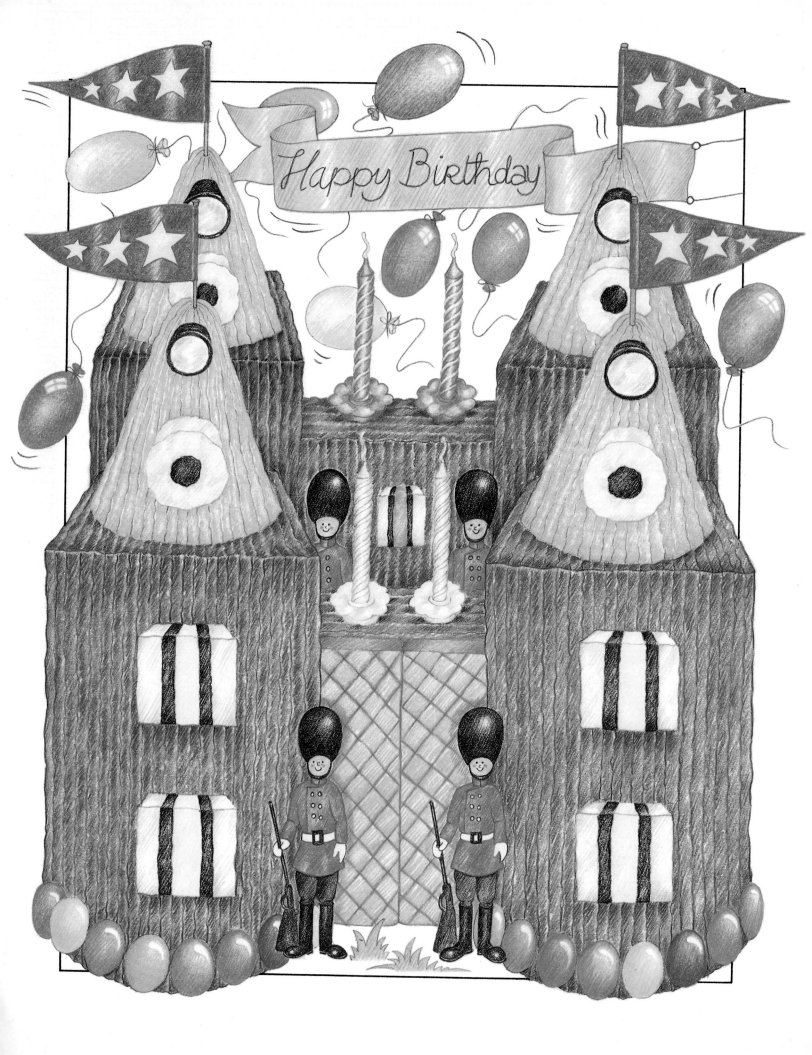

YOU WILL NEED

COCKTAIL STICKS
4 SWISS ROLLS
GREEN FOOD COLOURING
375 g (12 oz) BUTTER
4 ICE CREAM CONES
Icing Sugar
750 g (1.5 lb) ICING SUGAR
Raspberry JAM
GLUE
COCOA POWDER
1 PACKET TRIFLE SPONGES
SCRAPS OF PAPER
SCISSORS & GLUE
BISCUITS & SWEETS TO DECORATE
4 STRAWS

CASTLE CAKE

HOW TO MAKE

1 Cut a slice off each swiss roll and place one swiss roll upright in each corner of a tray or cake board to form the castle towers.

2 Break sponge trifles in half and put jam on 3 sides of them.

Place them between the swiss rolls to form the walls of the castle.

To secure the walls and towers firmly, push cocktail sticks through the sponge trifles into the swiss rolls.

4 Cream together icing sugar and butter in a bowl.

Divide the mixture into 2 bowls, putting two thirds of the icing in one bowl and a third in the other.

Add 2 tablespoons of cocoa powder or 3 tablespoons of drinking chocolate into the large bowl of icing.

Mix well.

3 Cut the tops off 4 ice cream cones.

Mix a couple of drops of green food colouring into the other bowl.

5 Cover the ice cream cones with green icing, and make lines on the icing with a fork.

Cover the entire cake, both the outside and inside of the towers and walls with chocolate icing. Again, draw lines on the icing with a fork.

6 Place an ice cream cone on top of each swiss roll to complete the towers. Place Smarties around the end of the castle. Add 2 wafer biscuits to the front for a door.

Make flags with straws and paper and stick one on each tower.

Stick sweets such as Liquorice Allsorts around the castle as windows and doors.

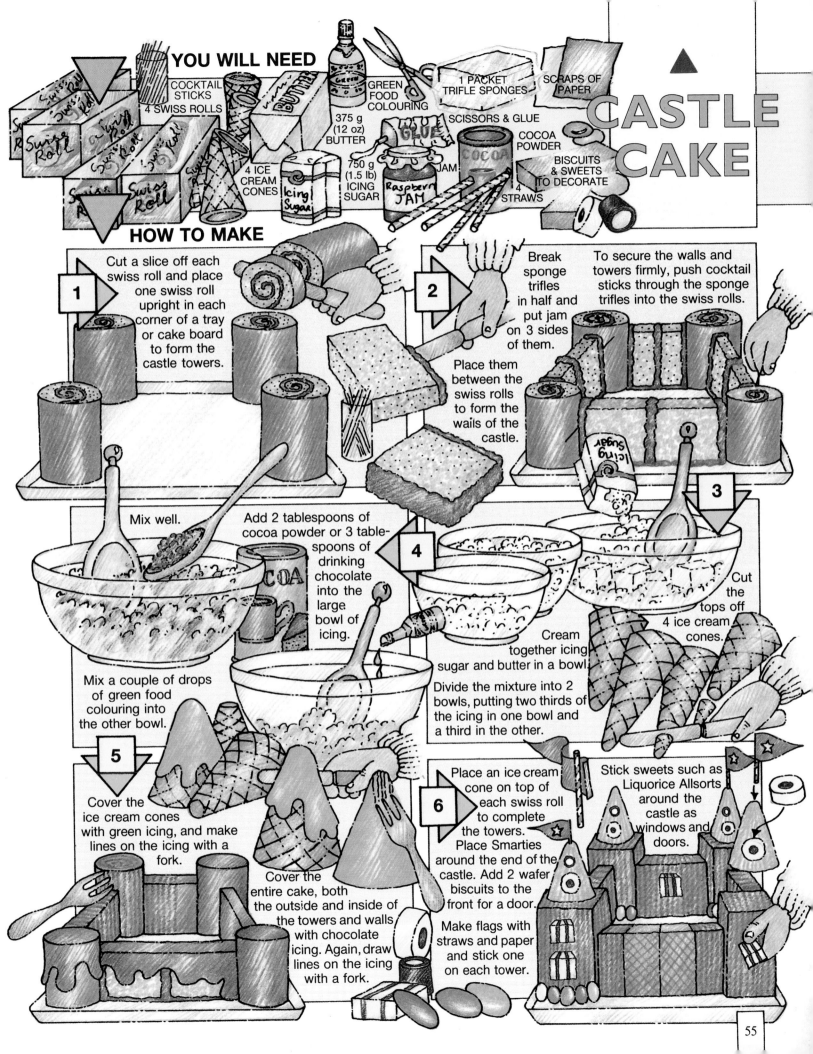

55

YOU WILL NEED

2–3 LARGE SHEETS CARDBOARD

VERY LARGE CARDBOARD BOX

1–2 SHEETS COLOURED PAPER

SCISSORS

STRING

PAINT & PAINT BRUSHES

PAINT

GLUE

HORSEBOXES

HOW TO MAKE

1 Cut a hole in the centre of the box big enough to fit over your head and body.

2 Paint the box or cover with coloured paper.

Decorate with cut out circles in different coloured paper.

Cut 6 long strips of paper for a tail. Curl them by pulling over a ruler and glue to back of box.

3 With scissors, make 2 small holes at either side of the big hole.

Thread 2 lengths of string through them so they fit over your shoulders and hold box at waist level.

Knot the string at the holes.

4 Draw the horse's head on cardboard, as in diagram. Cut out.

Draw and cut out a second one the same size.

Paint the heads the same colour as the horse's body or cover with coloured paper.

5 For a mane, cut several strips of paper the same length. Fold in half and glue to one side of the horse's head.

Glue the other horse's head to it.

Cut out eyes and ears from coloured paper and stick onto both sides of the horse's head.

6 With a craft knife or scissors, make a slit at the front of the box so that the horse's head fits into it and is attached to the body.

Cut a length of string for reins and thread through a hole in the horse's head.

57

YOU WILL NEED

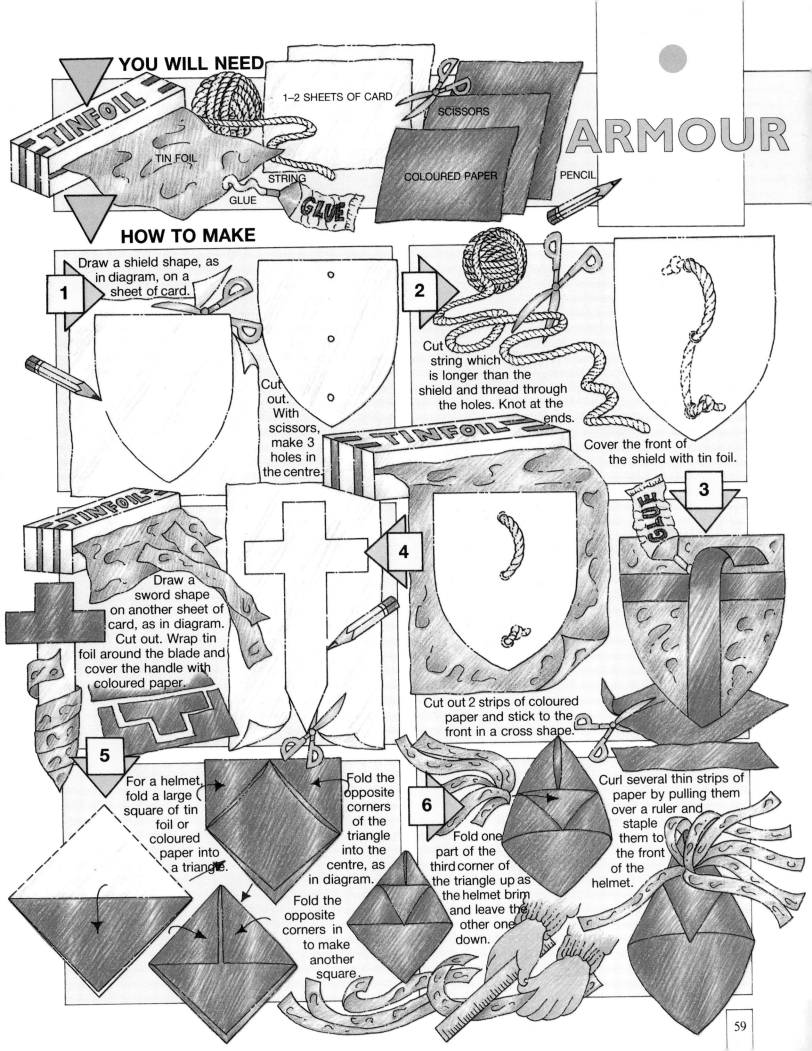

TINFOIL

TIN FOIL

1–2 SHEETS OF CARD

SCISSORS

STRING

GLUE

COLOURED PAPER

PENCIL

HOW TO MAKE

1 Draw a shield shape, as in diagram, on a sheet of card.

Cut out. With scissors, make 3 holes in the centre.

2 Cut string which is longer than the shield and thread through the holes. Knot at the ends.

Cover the front of the shield with tin foil.

3

4

Draw a sword shape on another sheet of card, as in diagram. Cut out. Wrap tin foil around the blade and cover the handle with coloured paper.

Cut out 2 strips of coloured paper and stick to the front in a cross shape.

5 For a helmet, fold a large square of tin foil or coloured paper into a triangle.

Fold the opposite corners of the triangle into the centre, as in diagram.

Fold the opposite corners in to make another square.

6 Fold one part of the third corner of the triangle up as the helmet brim and leave the other one down.

Curl several thin strips of paper by pulling them over a ruler and staple them to the front of the helmet.

YOU WILL NEED

CARD

MARKERS

SCISSORS   PENCIL

SMALL MAGNETS (AVAILABLE IN BUSINESS EQUIPMENT SHOPS)

FELT IN DIFFERENT COLOURS

GLUE

GLUE

FRIDGE MAGNETS

HOW TO MAKE

1 Draw lots of fruit shapes on card such as a banana, apple, orange, strawberry or pear. Cut them out.

2 Choose different coloured pieces of felt (such as yellow, red or orange) and stick the card fruit shapes onto them.

Cut them out.

3 With a black or brown marker, draw lines on the fruit to emphasise their shape.

4 Add felt leaves to the apples and pears and white spots to the strawberries.

Stick a magnet onto the back of each felt shape.

Put them on your fridge to hold messages, pictures or photographs.

5 You can also make other felt shapes such as a sun and moon.

Draw them on card first and cut out.

6 Again, glue the card shapes to felt pieces.

Cut out and outline with markers.

Stick a magnet to the back of the felt pieces and put on your fridge.

YOU WILL NEED

1–2 SHOE BOXES

SMALL BOXES AND BOTTLES

BLACK MARKER

4 TOILET ROLLS

Matches
LARGE MATCHBOX

2–3 SHEETS OF COLOURED PAPER & CARD

Poster Paint

Poster Paint

PAINT & PAINT BRUSHES

GLUE

SHOP

SCISSORS

HOW TO MAKE

1 Remove the shoe box lids.

Cover the boxes inside and out with coloured paper or paint them.

For the counter, cover a lid from one of the shoe boxes with coloured paper or paint it.

Do the same with the 4 toilet rolls.

2 For a shelf, place the top of the box on coloured card and draw around it.

Remove the box and draw a 2 cm edge around the rectangle.

Cut out.

For other shelves, repeat the process.

3 Make cuts in the shelf, as in diagram.

CUT   CUT   CUT   CUT

GLUE

4 Fold the edges down and glue at the corners. Put glue on 3 sides of the shelf and stick into the shoe box. You need 2 shelves for each box.

Fill them with small boxes and jars.

5 Glue a toilet roll into each of the 4 corners of the lid on the underside.

6 For a cash register, cut a long strip of paper 30 cm × 8 cm. Fold it in three and stick the paper in the centre on a large matchbox.

With a marker, draw dots in the middle like cash register keys.

£10

63

HELPFUL SUGGESTIONS

1. Be careful when using scissors or craft knife.

2. Have an adult present at all times when you are cooking or making the candles.

3. Use oven gloves to lift hot saucepans and tins.

4. Cover the area you are working on with old newspapers and, where possible, wear old clothes or an apron.

5. Some of the items are more difficult to make than others. The following symbols indicate the easy and more difficult ones:

   ● = Easy (6–9 years)   ▲ = Difficult (9–12 years)

6. There are lots of other symbols used throughout the book. This is what they mean:

   ✏ draw   🖌 paint   🧴 glue   ✂ cut   〜 sew

7. In a box or black sack, collect household rubbish such as cereal boxes, egg boxes, toilet rolls, yoghurt and cream cartons, bottles, newspapers, brown paper, old magazines, corks etc.

8. Use the measurements given where possible, especially when cooking.

9. Use an 'all purpose' glue for sticking most things, unless otherwise stated. Use poster and powder paint and washable markers where possible.

10. Do not forget to tidy up or there will not be much fun if others see the mess!

Mary Fitzgerald